20 EVENTS

Women

WHO ACHIEVED GREATNESS

CATHIE CUSH

RSVP

**RAINTREE
Steck-Vaughn**
PUBLISHERS
The Steck-Vaughn Company

Austin, Texas

Consultant: Gary Gerstle, Department of History, The Catholic University of America, Washington, D.C.

Developed for Steck-Vaughn Company by
Visual Education Corporation, Princeton, New Jersey

Project Director: Jewel Moulthrop
Editor: Michael Gee
Copy Editor: Margaret P. Roeske
Editorial Assistants: Carol Ciaston, Stacy Tibbetts
Photo Research: Martin A. Levick
Production Supervisor: Maureen Ryan Pancza
Proofreading Management: William A. Murray
Word Processing: Cynthia C. Feldner
Interior Design: Maxson Crandall, Lee Grabarczyk
Cover Design: Maxson Crandall
Page Layout: Maxson Crandall, Lisa Evans-Skopas, Christine Osborne

Raintree Steck-Vaughn Publishers staff

Editor: Shirley Shalit
Project Manager: Joyce Spicer

Library of Congress Cataloging-in-Publication Data

Cush, Cathie, 1957–
    Women who achieved greatness / Cathie Cush.
        p.   cm. — (20 Events)
    Includes bibliographical references and index.
    ISBN 0-8114-4938-6
    1. Women in public life—Biography—Juvenile literature.
2. Women in politics—Biography—Juvenile literature.
[1. Women—Biography.] I. Title. II. Series.
HQ1390.C87 1995
920.72—dc20
                                                   94–11307
                                                        CIP
                                                         AC

Cover: Eleanor Roosevelt served as a delegate to the United Nations General Assembly (inset) from 1945 to 1951. The U.N. building (background) is located in New York City.

Credits and Acknowledgments
Cover photos: George Holton/Photo Researchers, Inc. (background), Leo Rosenthal/FDR Library (inset)
Illustrations: Parrot Graphics, Precision Graphics

4: The Bettmann Archive (top), North American Montessori Teachers Association (bottom); **5:** Cliff Moore; **6:** Library of Congress; **7:** Perkins School for the Blind; **8:** FDR Library (top), FDR Library (bottom); **9:** FDR Library; **10:** Schlesinger Library, Radcliffe College; **11:** © 1937 *The New York Times*; **13:** ASAP/GPO; **15:** UPI/Bettmann (top), Library of Congress (bottom); **16:** Evelyn Keller/Cold Spring Harbor Laboratory Archives; **17:** UPI/Bettmann; **18:** AP/Wide World Photos; **19:** UPI/Bettmann (top), Wide World Photos (bottom); **20:** UPI/Bettmann; **21:** © Margaret Bourke-White/Life Magazine/Time Warner, Inc.; **22:** AP/Wide World Photos; **23:** Bill Silliker, Jr., Ocean Park, Maine; **24:** Perrin Carol/Gamma Liaison Network (top), J. P. Laffont/Sygma (bottom); **26:** Tom Hanley/Camera Press London/Globe Photos; **27:** AP/Wide World Photos; **28:** AP/Wide World Photos; **29:** Dennis Cooke/Wide World Photos; **30:** UPI/Bettmann; **31:** AP/Wide World Photos; **32:** Reuters/Bettmann; **33:** Reuters/Bettmann; **34:** Gerry Ellis, Portland, Oregon; **35:** S. Matthews/Jane Goodall Institute, Ridgefield, Connecticut; **36:** Dev O'Neill/The Barbara Jordan Archives, Texas Southern University; **37:** UPI/Bettmann; **39:** Dominic Faulder/Sygma; **40:** Courtesy Corporate Archives/Phillips Petroleum Company; **41:** Sammy Still/Cherokee Nation; **42:** AP/Wide World Photos; **43:** Michael Ferguson/Globe Photos

Contents

Maria Montessori

This Italian physician and educator revolutionized early childhood education with the method that bears her name.

In an early Montessori school in France, two children watch as a third child washes clothes. Later the clothes will be ironed, folded, and put away.

Exceptional Education

The modern nation of Italy was formed in 1870. That year, in the town of Chiaravalle, Maria Montessori was born—the daughter of a civil servant and his wife. When Maria was seven, the Italian government set up a new public education system and made primary school a requirement for both boys and girls.

Montessori was brought up to love learning, to help those less

Montessori's theories about education became the basis for many schools around the world.

fortunate than herself, and to do household chores. But as a student, she grew to dislike the Italian educational system, which encouraged all students to think alike. And she rebelled against the idea that a woman had only two career choices: homemaker or teacher.

Instead, Montessori became the first woman in Italy to earn a medical degree. After completing her studies, she established a school in Rome for retarded children. Using educational materials that she developed, Montessori taught her students much more than anyone expected. Her students easily passed the state exams for their primary education certificates—the average level of schooling for most Italians at the time. In 1900, Montessori began a seven-year program of study toward becoming a child psychiatrist.

The Montessori Method

A New School In January 1907, Montessori opened *Casa dei Bambini* (Children's House), a school for young children, in the poor San Lorenzo section of Rome. The people of the district welcomed the school because it gave their children someplace to go. Before the school was built, most young children were home alone while their parents worked. The school opened in one room of a low-income apartment building. About 60 students ranging in age from two and a half to seven years old attended. Parents earned the right to send their children to the school by helping to clean the building or working on other tasks. Montessori lived in the building herself and met with the parents each week.

Montessori, who was known as the *Dottoressa* (Doctor), used the methods that she had developed earlier. The children were not separated by age but were free to use all the resources in the classroom. Montessori set up various learning stations around the room. Children moved at their own pace from one station to another. At each station, Montessori presented them with materials designed to stimulate their interest without frustrating or boring them. Every activity had an educational purpose. The more senses that were involved in the activity, the better. For example, a game of blindman's buff was used to train children to use their senses of hearing and touch.

In addition to developing the senses, students learned mathematics, language, science, and geography skills as well as practical living skills such as washing, sweeping, preparing food, and dressing themselves. Montessori created learning aids that allowed the children to practice buttoning clothes and tying shoelaces.

Learning by Doing Montessori kept a variety of materials available so that the children could always find something that interested them. She eliminated equipment and activities that children did not like or use. Montessori believed that children became bored when they were made to do certain things, as she had been as a student. She also believed that a child stopped trying to learn when a teacher told the child that he or she was wrong. To avoid this, Montessori developed educational materials that the students could use to correct themselves, without the teacher. Learning was more effective, Montessori believed, when the child found and corrected his or her own mistakes.

Montessori's approach to reading and writing was unusual at the time. Her students began to learn to read and write before they reached the age of five. At first, they used sandpaper letters on smooth boards. The children traced the letters with their fingers. By the time the children started using pencils, the muscles of their hands were already familiar with the shapes of the letters. Next they used letter cards to make words. These steps helped

build the skills that the children would need to read and write. Montessori felt that the early exercises also gave the children the motivation and confidence to progress to more advanced skills.

Self-confidence was an important part of Montessori's program. So was self-discipline. Although the students moved about freely (making the classrooms seem unstructured), they had rules to follow. They learned at an early age to be responsible for themselves and to do their own work. In Montessori's classroom, the teacher observed and encouraged; the students—by doing—taught themselves.

> *"[Whoever] strives for the regeneration of education strives for the regeneration of the human race."*

In this quotation, Maria Montessori emphasizes that by reforming education we improve all humankind.

School for Success

After a successful year at *Casa dei Bambini,* Montessori opened a second school. Word of her method spread, and educators came from all over the world to learn about this remarkable new system. Several American educators were inspired by what they saw in Montessori's schools. In 1912, they organized the Child Education Foundation in New York City to put her principles to work. The foundation's director, Eva McLin, opened a Montessori nursery school in the United States in 1915.

Despite this early interest, however, the Montessori method did not become widely accepted among U.S. educators until the late 1950s. Since then, many private and public schools in the United States have adopted her methods. The first Montessori public elementary school opened in Cincinnati, Ohio, in 1975.

Maria Montessori fled Italy's Fascist government in 1934. She worked in Spain and Asia and finally settled in the Netherlands, where she lived until she died in 1952. The Montessori method is now used in thousands of schools around the world. Her philosophy has influenced all areas of education. Montessori's *Casa dei Bambini* was also a forerunner of today's day-care programs. Her teaching tools are the basis of many popular toys for toddlers.

Following Maria Montessori's principles, children in this present-day classroom learn mainly by teaching themselves.

Helen Keller and Annie Sullivan

A deaf and blind woman and her teacher changed the way the world looked at the disabled.

Helen Keller holds out her hand as her teacher, Annie Sullivan, uses the manual alphabet to spell the words in the book she is reading into Helen's hand.

Kindred Spirits

Annie Sullivan As a poor child growing up in Massachusetts, Anne Mansfield Sullivan was diagnosed with a disease that left her eyes puffy and cloudy. Sullivan's eyesight was so bad that she sometimes cut off the heads of her paper dolls by accident. A sympathetic and caring priest arranged for an operation to improve the young girl's sight.

In 1880, Sullivan entered the Perkins Institute for the Blind in Boston. She had frequent temper tantrums and earned her nickname "Miss Spitfire," until a kind and gentle teacher taught her about patience and self-respect. After several more eye operations, Sullivan was able to read. She completed her studies and, in 1886, she graduated at the head of her class.

Helen Keller The year Sullivan entered Perkins, Helen Adams Keller was born in a small town in northern Alabama. When she was 19 months old, a high fever left her deaf and blind. As a child, Keller often threw wild tantrums out of sheer frustration at her inability to understand her environment and to communicate.

When Helen was nearly seven, the Keller family began looking for a teacher for her. They contacted officials at the Perkins Institute, who recommended its recent graduate Annie Sullivan.

▶ In this excerpt, Helen Keller describes the moment when, as a young child, she made the connection between the world and the words Sullivan was spelling into her hand.

The Miracle Worker

On March 3, 1887, Helen Keller waited on the front porch for her teacher, Annie Sullivan, to arrive. Helen Keller later called it "the most important day I remember in all my life." When Sullivan arrived, she gave Keller a doll to gain her trust and cooperation. At the same time, she spelled the word d-o-l-l into Keller's hand using the manual alphabet. Unable to understand the "game," Keller grabbed the doll and smashed it.

Sullivan was surprised at how the family let Helen have her own way. At the table, Helen took food from everyone's plate. And Helen was not reprimanded when she pinched her new teacher. Sullivan knew that she needed to stand up to the unruly child and teach her some manners.

W-a-t-e-r Sullivan found it hard to make progress in the presence of the family, who stepped in whenever Helen had a temper tantrum. Sullivan asked for a place where she and Helen could be by themselves. They were given the use of a garden house. Away from the family, their progress was astonishing. Within days, Keller was learning to sew, knit, and string beads. Sullivan continued to spell words into Keller's hands, but Helen was confused. The spelling exercise was still only a game to her. Although she learned the alphabet, she did not yet associate the letters with words and their meanings.

Then one day, as Keller was washing her hands, she patted Sullivan's

> "She placed my hand under the water spout. As the cool stream gushed over one hand she spelled 'water' into the other. Suddenly the mystery of language was revealed to me. I knew then that 'w-a-t-e-r' meant the wonderful cool something that was flowing over my hand. That living word awakened my soul, gave it light, hope, joy, set it free! There were barriers still, it is true, but barriers that could in time be swept away."
>
> —From *The Story of My Life*

hand. It was her way of asking for the word for something she was touching. Sullivan took Keller to the garden and put her hand into the cold water flowing from the pump. Into Keller's other hand, Sullivan spelled w-a-t-e-r. Suddenly Keller realized what the word meant. She asked Sullivan's name, and Sullivan spelled t-e-a-c-h-e-r. This breakthrough occurred less than a month after Sullivan had arrived at the Keller house.

Within an hour, Helen learned 30 words. She learned 5 or 6 new ones each day. With each new word, her world expanded. The easiest words to learn were ones that described objects, actions, or things that Keller could smell or taste. It was harder for Sullivan to explain words like "love," but Keller eventually realized that her feelings also had names.

Teacher and Her Student Keller's lessons were informal. She constantly asked questions, and Sullivan explained everything to her in great detail. After a while, Sullivan taught her braille, a special system of raised writing that allows blind people to read with their fingers.

Sullivan recorded the progress of her extraordinary student and sent a report to Perkins. When the institute published it, the pair became celebrities. Even Grover Cleveland,

who was U.S. President at that time, wanted to meet them.

Finding a Voice With Sullivan's help, Keller learned to use her voice to speak. (Children usually learn to speak by imitating the sounds they hear. Therefore, learning to speak is very difficult for deaf people.) Keller went to Perkins, where she was able to meet and communicate with other blind children. She also began formal lessons in history and other subjects.

In 1900, Keller entered Radcliffe College with Annie Sullivan at her side. If books were not available in braille, Sullivan would read them and spell them into Keller's hand. She did the same at lectures. For the next four years, the two worked very hard.

When Keller's English professor told a popular women's magazine about her remarkable student, the magazine asked Keller to write articles for them. At age 22, Helen Keller wrote *The Story of My Life*. Following Keller's graduation, she and Annie Sullivan settled on a farm in Massachusetts, where they lived with Sullivan's husband (and Keller's editor), John Macy.

Throughout her life, Keller worked to help other deaf and blind people. She is shown here reading a book printed in braille.

Spreading the Word

In 1914, in order to support themselves and increase awareness of the needs of disabled people, Keller and Sullivan began lecturing across the United States and, later, in Europe. In 1924, they began raising funds for the American Foundation for the Blind. They also supported a program to record books for the blind. As a result of their efforts, the government gave 23,000 phonographs to blind people through the program.

Parted Friends After Annie Sullivan died in 1936, Keller wrote that "She opened the locked gates of my being, and I stretched out my hands in the quest of life." Keller continued to work on behalf of the disabled, particularly with soldiers who had been blinded during World War II.

Helen Keller wrote several books about her life experiences and beliefs. Keller and Sullivan were also the subject of others' books and movies, including the successful 1962 film *The Miracle Worker*, written by William Gibson.

Helen Keller died in 1968 at the age of 88. Her life and work continue to inspire people with and without disabilities.

Eleanor Roosevelt

❧

She redefined the role of First Lady and advocated the rights of women, minorities, and the poor.

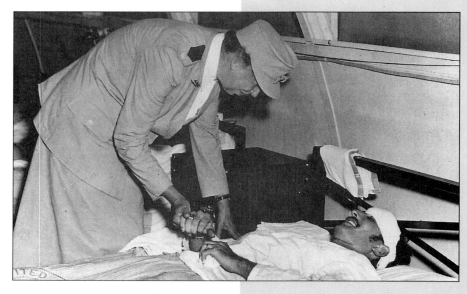

Eleanor Roosevelt talks with a wounded soldier in the Pacific during World War II.

Age of Innocence

Anna Eleanor Roosevelt, one of the greatest advocates for the poor and downtrodden, had an upper-class childhood. She was born in New York City in 1884 and was raised by her grandmother from the age of ten, when her parents died. Her uncle was Theodore Roosevelt, 26th President of the United States.

Another Side of Life At boarding school in London, Eleanor Roosevelt

Even as a young woman, Eleanor Roosevelt knew she wanted to help those who were less fortunate.

met Marie Souvestre, whose father was a philosopher in favor of radical social and political changes. Roosevelt came to share his belief that some things in life were more important than society parties. At age 18, she went to work for the National Consumer's League, an organization that promoted health and safety for factory workers, especially women.

Entering Politics In 1905, Eleanor Roosevelt married a cousin, Franklin Delano Roosevelt (FDR). Together, they had six children. While FDR embarked on a political career in New York State, Eleanor dropped out of public life to raise her children. But during World War I, she volunteered with the Red Cross and the League of Women Voters. After her husband was stricken with polio (a crippling disease) in 1921, Eleanor Roosevelt became more involved in politics.

In Her Own Right

Eleanor Roosevelt first entered the political world on behalf of her husband. While performing his duties for the New York Democratic Party, she began mobilizing people behind reform causes. At the 1924 Democratic convention, she led a group that promoted a party program that would include tougher child labor standards, equal pay for women, and other women's reform issues. Although the effort was not successful, Eleanor Roosevelt became recognized as a skillful and determined organizer.

During the 1920s, Eleanor Roosevelt was active in the League of Women Voters and the Women's Trade Union League as well as the Democratic Party. By the 1928 election year, she had become a political figure in her own right as head of the Women's Division of the Democratic Party. In the 1932 election, when her husband ran for President, she continued to lead the Democratic women.

The White House When FDR was elected president in 1932, Eleanor Roosevelt feared that she would become little more than a White House hostess. Instead, she started her own radio show and wrote a regular newspaper column. She brought many women activists to Washington. She boosted the status of women reporters by holding press conferences for women only. She made sure that the President's "New Deal" programs, designed to relieve the hardships of the Great Depression, included benefits for women. In 1936, the Democratic Platform Committee addressed many women's issues, thanks to the efforts of Eleanor Roosevelt.

One of the reasons why Eleanor Roosevelt was so influential was that she had direct access to a very popular President. If she had a cause or idea she wanted to promote, she could arrange the seating at a state dinner, for example, so that someone who supported her position sat next to the President. One newspaper columnist, likening her influence to that of a cabinet member, called her "the most influential woman of our times."

Underdogs Eleanor Roosevelt always supported those who had suffered injustice. She made the civil rights of African Americans an important issue in the White House, and she practiced what she believed. In 1939, she attended the Birmingham Southern Conference on Human Welfare. The lecture hall was supposed to be segregated, with blacks sitting in

Eleanor Roosevelt's Life and Work	
1884	Born on October 11
1905	Married Franklin Delano Roosevelt (FDR)
1921	Became active in League of Women Voters, Women's Trade Union League, and Women's Division of Democratic Party
1924	Cofounded furniture factory to help unemployed workers
1928	Became head of Women's Division of Democratic Party
1933	Became First Lady as FDR began first term as President
1935	Began newspaper column called "My Day"
1939	Resigned from DAR to protest its refusal to allow Marian Anderson to sing in Constitution Hall
1945	Appointed one of first five delegates to United Nations; helped write Universal Declaration of Human Rights
1952	Resigned from UN
1961	Reappointed to UN by President Kennedy
1962	Died on November 7

one half and whites in the other. Roosevelt moved her chair so that she straddled the dividing line. She joined the National Association for the Advancement of Colored People, the leading black civil rights organization. She also withdrew her membership in the Daughters of the American Revolution when the group prohibited Marian Anderson, an African American singer, from performing in Constitution Hall.

Roosevelt's causes included the rights of young people and the plight of Jewish refugees fleeing Nazi Germany. She traveled extensively during World War II, visiting American troops fighting in Europe.

Throughout her life, Eleanor Roosevelt was respected for her hard work and commitment.

Peace Ambassador

Eleanor Roosevelt stayed active in politics even after FDR's death in 1945. She wanted to see his New Deal policies continued. President Harry Truman nominated her as the U.S. delegate to the United Nations, where she helped draft its Universal Declaration of Human Rights. When the declaration passed the General Assembly on December 10, 1948, the members recognized her three-year effort with a standing ovation.

In the 1950s, Roosevelt spent several years traveling around the world to promote peace. In 1962, she sponsored hearings on civil rights in Washington, D.C. President John F. Kennedy made her chairperson of his Commission on the Status of Women, her last official position.

Eleanor Roosevelt died on November 7, 1962. As a strong advocate of social change, she touched millions of lives and showed people the possibilities for improvement.

After her husband's death, Eleanor Roosevelt continued to meet with world leaders. She is shown here with India's prime minister, Jawaharlal Nehru.

9

Amelia Earhart

~~~~~~~~~~

A pioneer aviator, she was the first woman to make a solo flight across the Atlantic Ocean.

An Interest in Flying

Amelia Mary Earhart was born in Kansas just before the turn of the 20th century. She was barely five years old when Orville and Wilbur Wright made their famous flight at Kitty Hawk, North Carolina. She would grow up to make aviation history of her own.

Earhart was a bright student, even though she sometimes rebelled against her teachers. While she was in school, she started saving newspaper clippings about women who were the first to break into traditional male positions, such as bank president and U.S. Civil Service commissioner. After high school, Earhart attended several colleges and worked at a variety of jobs in search of a satisfying career. It was during this time that flying caught her attention.

In 1920, Earhart accompanied her father to an air show celebrating the opening of an airfield in Long Beach, California. Earhart was fascinated by the exhibition of stunt flyers who raced and performed wing-walking and other midair acrobatic tricks. Three days after the show, Earhart's father bought her a ticket for a plane ride.

That ride was to change Amelia Earhart's life. As she later recalled, "As soon as we left the ground, I knew I myself had to fly."

To Fly!

Pilots were rare in the early days of flying—and women pilots were rarer. In 1919, an American named Laura Brownell became the world's first licensed female pilot. In January 1921, Earhart started her flying lessons with another woman, Neta Snook. Earhart worked at odd jobs to pay for the training, which cost $1 for each minute. She had to take a streetcar and then walk three miles to reach the airfield for her lessons.

Earhart set a women's altitude record—14,000 feet without bottled oxygen—while still a student pilot. This would be the first of many aviation milestones. When she received her pilot's license on May 15, 1923, she was just shy of her 26th birthday. She was one of only 16 licensed female pilots in the world.

Atlantic Crossings In 1927, after Charles Lindbergh made the first solo flight across the Atlantic, publisher and promoter (organizer of special events) George Palmer Putnam asked Earhart to accompany two male aviators on a transatlantic flight. Although she would not actually fly the plane, Earhart would gain fame as the first woman to fly the Atlantic. She made the flight from Newfoundland, Canada, to Wales in Great Britain in July 1928 and received a hero's welcome on her return.

Earhart married Putnam in 1931. That spring, she began preparing for a solo transatlantic flight. No one had yet duplicated Lindbergh's feat.

Earhart left Teterboro, New Jersey, on May 19, 1932, and flew to Saint John, New Brunswick, in Canada. The

In this 1926 photo, Amelia Earhart is shown in the cockpit of her training plane.

This is an excerpt from a letter that Amelia Earhart wrote to her father shortly before she took off on her last and fatal flight.

next evening, on the fifth anniversary of Lindbergh's flight, she took off for Paris. After only four hours in the air, Earhart encountered a severe storm. Two navigational gauges in her aircraft failed, so she had no way of knowing if she was still on course. Then her fuel gauge broke. But the closest landing field in Newfoundland had no lights. Earhart knew that she would never find her way back in the dark. She continued east. Just after dawn, she spotted land and came down near Londonderry, Ireland.

Earhart was mobbed by reporters and well-wishers. Telegrams congratulating her came from all over the world. Upon her return to New York, a celebration was held in her honor. The National Geographic Society gave her a gold medal—the first ever awarded to a woman.

For days and weeks after Earhart's disappearance, headlines like this one occupied the front pages of many newspapers.

The Final Flight

Earhart continued to fly and set new records. Hungry for a new challenge, she decided to circle the world near the equator—a 28,595-mile series of flights. In early 1937, she flew alone from Oakland, California, to Honolulu, Hawaii. Mechanical trouble grounded her in Hawaii. The plane was repaired, and Earhart was ready to try again.

Later that same year, Earhart and her navigator, Frederick Noonan, left from Miami, Florida, and flew down to South America and across the Atlantic to Africa. She had to pilot around tornadoes and sandstorms in the Sahara Desert. When Earhart's plane crossed the Arabian Sea on June 15, the fliers had covered 15,000 miles. They continued on to India, Singapore, Indonesia, and then Australia.

Last Leg After reaching Papua New Guinea, Earhart and Noonan took off on July 2, 1937, at 10:22 A.M. They were to navigate 2,500 miles over open ocean to Howland Island, on the equator just east of the International Date Line. At 6:15 the next morning, Earhart radioed the U.S. Coast Guard cutter *Itasca* that her plane was only 200 miles from Howland.

At 7:41 A.M. she told the cutter crew, "We must be on you, but cannot see you. Gas is running low."

At 7:50 A.M.: "We are circling, but cannot hear you."

At 8:45 A.M.: "We are on the line 157/337."

It was the last message received from Amelia Earhart.

The Search Ten ships and 65 planes covered 50,000 square miles—an area of ocean the size of Texas—in an exhaustive 16-day search for Earhart's plane. Neither the plane nor its fliers were found, although the search was very thorough.

More than 30 years after Earhart disappeared, people were still trying to solve the mystery. Richard Gillespie, an aircraft historian, put together a team to renew the search. Using navigational information to recreate Earhart's flight, Gillespie's team came to the island of Nikumaroro, just south of the equator, not far from Howland. There they found some artifacts, including a navigator's bookcase and part of a woman's shoe. These items may be all that remains from the final flight of a brave woman and an aviation pioneer.

11

Golda Meir

A leader of the Zionist movement, she worked for Israeli statehood and served as prime minister.

Homelands

The story of Golda Meir is intertwined with the histories of the Jewish people and of Israel. Over 3,000 years ago, Jews first established a kingdom in Palestine with Jerusalem as its capital. Over time, however, conflicts with other groups forced most Jews to leave the region. Many migrated to Europe and Russia.

Fear and Persecution Prejudice against Jews, or anti-Semitism, dates back centuries. Many early Christians blamed the Jews for the Roman crucifixion of Jesus. Others hated Jews because they were "different."

The woman who would one day help to establish a Jewish nation experienced that prejudice. Golda Mabovitch was born in 1898 into a poor family in Kiev, a city in the Ukraine. Her father, who was a carpenter, sometimes was not paid for his work because he was a Jew. In the Russian Empire (which included the Ukraine), this kind of treatment was legal. Jewish people lived in fear of pogroms, or organized massacres, which erupted frequently in the Ukraine and other areas.

A New Land To escape these hardships, the Mabovitch family emigrated to the United States in 1906. Golda was an excellent student and later studied to be a teacher. She also became involved in the movement called Zionism, based on the Old Testament name for Jerusalem. Zionists wanted to form a Jewish state in Palestine, where they could live free of anti-Semitism.

An Old Home In 1917, Great Britain took control of Palestine and promised Zionist leaders that it would support a Jewish homeland there. Jews from around the world began moving to Palestine. By 1939, nearly 400,000 Jews had settled there. But Palestine was also home to many Arab peoples, as it had been for centuries. The Arabs resented the influx of Jews. Arabs and Jews disagreed so violently over who had the right to be in Palestine that a British army had to struggle to maintain peace.

In 1921, Golda and her husband, Morris Myerson, moved to Palestine with a group of Zionists. (She changed her name to the Hebrew form of Myerson—Meir—in 1956.) They were among the earliest Jewish pioneers. First, the Myersons worked on a kibbutz, a communal farm where everyone took turns doing different jobs. Many of these farm communities were established by Jews settling in Palestine. After two years, the couple moved to Tel Aviv, where Golda worked as a clerk, took in washing, and became involved in the labor movement. During the 1930s, she represented Jewish labor organizations at several international conferences. She also became active in the World Zionist Organization, which continued to strive for Jewish statehood. Eventually, Golda Meir became the

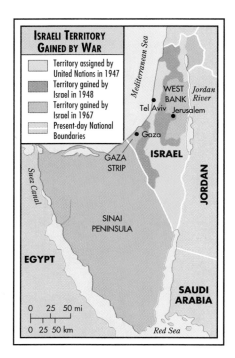

By defeating attacks from neighboring Arab countries, Israel added to its territory.

spokesperson to the world for the Jews of Palestine.

Increasing Threats Resentment against the Jews grew. Arab revolts in 1929 and 1936 killed many Jews and destroyed property. But prejudice and fear were also on the rise outside the Middle East. In Germany in the 1930s, Nazi dictator Adolf Hitler blamed many social problems on the Jews. He claimed that contact with the Jews had soiled the pure German race.

By the end of World War II, six million Jews—one-third of the world's Jewish population—had been exterminated by Hitler's Nazis. Many died in concentration camps. To Jews and many other people around the world, these events made the formation of a Jewish state more critical than ever. After the war, Golda Meir led many delegations abroad to raise international support for the cause of Jewish statehood.

Golda Meir shakes hands with other officials as the Proclamation of Independence is signed and Israel becomes a Jewish homeland.

Birth of a Nation

In 1947, the work of Meir and the other Zionist leaders paid off. The United Nations decided to create two states in Palestine—one for Jews and one for Arabs. The Arabs rejected this plan, and fighting broke out. Meir traveled to the United States and Great Britain to raise money to fight back. People were so moved by her tales of Palestinian Jews standing in line for hours to donate blood for their soldiers that she was able to raise $50 million to equip an army.

Independence On May 14, 1948, British troops left Palestine, and Jewish leaders declared the new country of Israel. Golda Meir was among the signers of the Proclamation of Independence. As one of Israel's ablest diplomats, Meir was named the nation's first ambassador to the Soviet Union. She was also elected to the Israeli parliament. After establishing ties with Russia, she left that post to become the first minister of labor and social insurance. In that post, she instituted a national health insurance program. She also directed the construction of new housing at a time when more than 1,000 immigrants were arriving in Israel each day.

After seven years as labor minister, Meir was appointed minister of foreign affairs. Although Meir always endorsed diplomacy, she also favored a strong military and a policy of reacting quickly to Arab threats.

A New Leader After ten years as foreign minister, Meir left the government. But her retirement was short-lived. In 1969, Golda Meir became prime minister. Tension was extremely high between Israel and its Arab neighbors. During a six-day war in 1967, Israel had captured much Arab territory. Small battles continued to erupt in these areas. The region and the world were weary of war. Meir wanted to find peace, but she refused to back down to Arab threats.

Just before dawn on October 6, 1973, Egypt and Syria attacked Israel by surprise. It was Yom Kippur (the Day of Atonement), the holiest day of the Jewish year. Although the Arab soldiers greatly outnumbered the Israelis, Jewish troops rallied. A cease-fire was signed on October 24.

Although Israel did not lose ground, many Israelis criticized Meir for being unprepared for the attack. Her popularity dropped, and she resigned several months later.

Golda Meir's Legacy

Golda Meir died of cancer in 1978. Just four months after her death, representatives from Egypt and Israel signed a peace agreement ending 30 years of hostility.

Meir, "the architect of Israel's diplomacy," was known for both her toughness and her warm personality. She was a grandmother and an international stateswoman, a world leader who held policy discussions over a cup of coffee in her kitchen. In her lifetime, she helped shape a modern nation.

> **"Can we from now on, all of us, turn a new leaf, and instead of fighting among each other can we all, united, fight poverty, disease, illiteracy? Can we, is it possible for us to pool all our efforts, all our energy, for one single purpose—the betterment and progress and development of all our lands and all our peoples?"**
>
> —**Address to the United Nations, 1957**

Meir always preferred diplomacy when dealing with Israel's enemies. In these words, she expressed the hope that Jews and Arabs will be able to work together for their mutual benefit.

Margaret Mead

Her famous studies of Pacific islanders challenged the traditional ideas of male and female roles in society.

PACIFIC OCEAN

13°S

Savaii

WESTERN SAMOA

Upolu

New Guinea

AUSTRALIA

PACIFIC OCEAN

Area Shown

14°S

Tutuila

Ofu

Olosega

Tau

0 10 20 mi

0 10 20 km

AMERICAN SAMOA

172°W   171°W   170°W   169°W

For her first study site, Mead chose Samoa, a U.S. possession in the Pacific.

Coming of Age in America

Margaret Mead was born in Philadelphia in 1901, one of five children. Her mother, Emily Fogg Mead, was a social scientist who worked with immigrants and supported women's rights. She taught Margaret understanding for the differences among peoples. She said that sometimes people behaved differently because they had had different experiences.

Margaret Mead acquired her mother's interest in studying people. While attending Barnard College in New York City, Mead studied Native American religion and culture under Franz Boas and his assistant, Ruth Benedict. Boas was exploring a brand new field of research—cultural anthropology (the study of human cultures). Mead continued her studies at Columbia University, earning advanced degrees in psychology and anthropology.

Mead found that Boas and Benedict were guided by the same humane principles that her family had instilled in her. They questioned many traditional ideas in American society that they felt were misguided.

One was that women were by nature less capable of doing most jobs and were therefore secondary to men. Another was that sex, although part of life, should not be openly discussed, especially with children. Boas, Benedict, and Mead were also alarmed by the rising tide of racism and prejudice against immigrants in 1920s America. Beneath these common attitudes lay the widespread belief that the peoples of Western Europe and their descendants in the United States were superior to all others. Some social scientists supported this belief with the assertion that certain peoples were superior to others by nature or by heredity.

Mead, like her teachers, felt that careful scientific investigation of other cultures could challenge these ideas. Viewing other cultures for what they are rather than through the distorting lens of Western beliefs could provide great insights into the human condition. Mead wanted to show the importance of culture and upbringing—"nurture" rather than "nature"—in shaping how people behave and what they believe in.

South Pacific

Mead decided to study how teenage females developed differently in different cultures. She planned to carry out part of her research in the United States and the other part on a primitive island in French Polynesia, in the South Pacific. Then she could compare the two cultures.

Professor Boas feared that a tropical island in the South Pacific would be too dangerous for this small, 23-year-old woman to spend nine months. Boas felt that it would be safer for Mead to study in a place where she could have some contact with her own civilization. Boas and Mead finally agreed on American Samoa, a U.S. possession in the South Pacific. English missionaries had visited these islands for more than a century, and the U.S. Navy had a base there.

Mead chose to do her research on Tau, one of the more remote islands in the group. The villagers on Tau followed traditional customs. They spoke no English. They built beehive-shaped huts out of coral rubble from the sea, with woven blinds as walls. They fished and gathered food and did some farming.

Coming of Age in Samoa Mead observed that, in contrast to modern American society, adolescence was not a difficult time for young Samoan women. Young Samoan girls had to tend babies, clean, and do household chores. But when these girls reached 14, they were free to learn other adult skills such as weaving and planting. They were also sexually aware from an early age, so that sex was not thought of as something secret.

Mead returned to New York in 1926. She published the results of her fieldwork in *Coming of Age in Samoa*. This was her first and still most famous book. In it, Mead concluded that the United States had much to learn from Samoan culture. She felt that Samoan children benefited from being raised in an extended family, where many adults—such as grandparents, aunts and uncles, and family friends—contributed to their upbringing. She also agreed with the Samoan tradition of expecting young girls to work. She believed that working gave them a feeling of purpose that was important to their well-being.

Mead's study was unique because, unlike earlier researchers, she made women her focus. Most cultural studies had centered on male roles and behavior.

In 1931, Mead traveled to New Guinea to study male and female gender roles in primitive cultures. She found that, in one group, both men and women were gentle and nurturing. In another, both sexes were aggressive. In a third, the women were businesslike and the men were artistic. Through her findings, Mead showed that personality traits usually associated with men or women are not determined by biological differences. Instead, male and female roles are shaped by culture and upbringing.

A Family Focus In New Guinea, Mead met another anthropologist, Gregory Bateson, whom she later married. The couple did fieldwork together in Bali and New Guinea, pioneering the use of photography to document the cultures they studied. When their daughter was born in 1939, Mead turned to a large network of friends to help raise the child. By doing so, she re-created the extended families she had studied in the islands.

In 1971, Mead helped organize an exhibit of items that she had collected in the Pacific.

Praise and Criticism

Margaret Mead encouraged people to be more accepting of different ways of life. Because of her ideas, many people saw Mead as a pioneer of modern feminism. Although Mead never called herself a feminist, she believed that women could both be mothers and have careers. Margaret Mead died in 1978.

During the 1980s, Mead's work became controversial. Some critics blamed her for the permissive attitudes of American society, particularly regarding sexual behavior. The controversy became so heated that it was even debated on *Donahue* (a television talk show), and Mead's daughter appeared on the show to defend her. Academics still debate whether Mead painted an accurate picture of island life or whether she saw there what she wanted to see. But most anthropologists agree that Margaret Mead made a major contribution to our understanding of the peoples of the world.

Margaret Mead admired much about the people whose cultures she studied. She is shown here with a Samoan woman.

Barbara McClintock

~~~~~

This Nobel Prize–winning geneticist opened the door to understanding heredity.

A New Breed of Woman

From an early age, Barbara McClintock had been interested in nature. Born in 1902 to a Connecticut physician and his wife, she often visited relatives in the Massachusetts countryside. When she was a young girl, her family moved to the Flatbush section of Brooklyn, New York, which at that time was still fairly rural. McClintock enjoyed outdoor activities, but she also liked to spend time reading alone. Although her parents encouraged their children to pursue their own interests, McClintock's mother sometimes worried that her daughter was too interested in books and nature and not in the things that girls were "supposed to do."

For one thing, Barbara McClintock wanted to go to college, but her parents refused to send her. Eventually, her persistence changed their minds. In 1919, McClintock enrolled in Cornell University to study biology. Some researchers there were pioneering in the field of genetics, the study of how offspring inherit characteristics from their parents. McClintock did so well in an undergraduate genetics course that she was invited to take graduate-level courses in her junior year. She went on to earn a Ph.D. in botany (the study of plants) from Cornell in 1927.

Corn Is the Key

Chromosomes and Genes At the time Barbara McClintock began her work in genetics, the field was young but progressing rapidly. Scientists had determined that

- Hereditary information is carried on structures called chromosomes inside each cell.
- Each chromosome contains many genes that control specific traits.
- In reproduction, the genetic information on the chromosomes of each parent combines to form a unique new genetic code for the offspring.

Genes were envisioned as beads on the strings of chromosomes. But no one had ever actually seen a chromosome or gene or understood how they worked inside the cell.

McClintock focused her lifelong research on wild corn, or maize. Its colorful kernels and leaves made it easy to see similarities and differences in each generation of plants. But working with corn also took planning and patience as the crop was planted, harvested, and studied each year.

Early Breakthroughs In 1924, McClintock developed a way to study individual maize chromosomes under a microscope and identify them by their shape and other characteristics. In breeding experiments, she

McClintock's work was so advanced that some scientists had difficulty understanding it. Fortunately, she persevered and in the end made a discovery that led to a greater understanding of some human diseases.

could then compare changes in the characteristics of the maize plants to changes on their chromosomes. This made it possible for the first time to identify which chromosomes carried the genes for particular traits. While still a graduate student, McClintock had developed a major new tool for genetic researchers.

Armed with this new technique, McClintock and her colleagues were able to prove a theory that parts of chromosomes broke off and reattached to other chromosomes during the formation of eggs and sperm. The theory helped explain why certain hereditary features vary among generations. McClintock's work in the 1930s and the early 1940s earned her recognition in the field and a succession of research grants and university positions.

Jumping Genes In the early 1940s, McClintock moved to the Carnegie Institute in Cold Spring Harbor, New York. There she made her most remarkable discovery. During her years of research, McClintock had been noting the many mutations, or genetic changes, that occurred in maize plants from one generation to the next. These changes often were not consistent with the known laws of genetics. Sometimes, mutations would occur and then disappear. Sometimes, changes would appear during a plant's development. McClintock suspected that some yet undetected activity was occurring on the chromosomes. She began to focus her experiments on discovering what it was.

McClintock worked on the puzzle for six years. Eventually, she discovered that there are certain elements on chromosomes that control genes. These "controlling elements," as McClintock called them,

On hearing the news that she had just won the Nobel Prize in physiology (the science of life processes), Barbara McClintock holds up an ear of corn for photographers.

either activate a gene so that its trait appears or suppress it so that the trait does not appear. Moreover, the controlling elements move around on the chromosome as the organism develops. McClintock called this "transposition."

The existence of these elements helped to answer many earlier unanswered questions about living things, including how they develop from one cell into complex bodies of many types of cells and how new species arise.

A Disappointing Reaction When McClintock presented the results of her work in 1951, they were not well received. The idea of mobile genetic elements, or "jumping genes," as they were called, contradicted many accepted beliefs, including the belief that genes remained fixed in place along chromosomes. Many scientists dismissed her old-fashioned study methods at a time when the most promising areas of genetics involved chemistry and physics. In actuality, her results were so far advanced that few researchers understood them. Because she worked alone, she had no one to back her up. And McClintock faced another obstacle: she was a woman in a field dominated by men. Discouraged by the lack of support, McClintock stopped publishing her research.

Well-Deserved Recognition
It was not until the 1970s that the importance of McClintock's work was recognized. By then, many other scientists were arriving at the same conclusions. She was awarded the Nobel Prize for physiology in 1983—more than 30 years after she presented her original research. She also received many other awards and recognition for her work, including the prestigious MacArthur Laureate Award. This gave her $60,000 a year tax free, for life, to enable her to carry out her work.

Barbara McClintock died in 1992. Her pioneering work in genetics helped us understand many things, including how resistance to antibiotics can be passed from one kind of bacteria to another. The concept has also paved the way for genetic engineers to identify genetic markers for hereditary diseases.

A scientist ahead of her time, McClintock based her work on knowledge and intuition. A lifetime of study and her "feeling for the organism" helped her discover more about how living organisms change and adapt.

Marian Anderson

⌒⌒⌒

As the first African American to sing at the Metropolitan Opera, she helped break the color barrier in the performing arts.

A Little Light Shines

Marian Anderson was born at the turn of the century, less than 40 years after President Abraham Lincoln freed the slaves. Anderson was just six years old when she started singing in the choir at the Union Baptist Church in Philadelphia. It was clear even then that this little girl had an extraordinary voice. At 13, she joined the church's senior choir and learned to sing different voice parts. Anderson was a contralto, having the lowest range of female singing voice.

The Anderson family did not have much money. Marian's father died when she was still a young girl. Her mother, a schoolteacher, took in laundry to make extra money. Still there was not enough money to pay for voice lessons for the young singer. The church congregation recognized Anderson's talent and took up a collection for her. But when Anderson approached the local music school, she was turned away because she was African American. Eventually, Anderson studied under Giuseppe Boghetti, a well-known voice teacher in New York City. He was so impressed by her talent that he taught her without charge for a year. Under his guidance, she won several prizes and scholarships for her singing.

A Singing Sensation

In 1930, Anderson performed in Europe for the first of many times. Although she was unknown when she arrived there, her warm, rich, velvety voice drew ovations across the continent. In Vienna, Austria, she began her concert to a half-empty theater. But word of her talent spread so fast that the theater was filled after intermission. When the great Italian conductor Arturo Toscanini heard Anderson, he said, "She has a voice that comes once in a hundred years."

When Anderson sang in Paris, she attracted the attention of Sol Hurok, a famous concert promoter. Hurok became Anderson's exclusive agent and arranged for her to make her U.S. debut at Town Hall in New York City on New Year's Eve 1935. Anderson did the show even though she had just broken her foot. The reviewers called her voice "stunning." The concerts she gave at Carnegie Hall that year sold out.

Let Freedom Sing Anderson was a hardworking professional. She continued to perform around the world. Between 1937 and 1938, she gave 70 performances in the United States. At the time, it was the most intensive recital schedule ever executed by a classical singer.

Many of the concert halls in the South where Anderson sang were segregated. Whites and blacks were seated separately: white ticket buyers

In 1939, Anderson sang on the steps of the Lincoln Memorial. She later described the importance of the event in her autobiography.

> *"I could see that my significance as an individual was small in this affair. I had become, whether I liked it or not, a symbol, representing my people."*
>
> —From *My Lord, What a Morning*

In 1961, Marian Anderson was asked to sing the national anthem at the inauguration of President John F. Kennedy. She is shown here with President Kennedy (*left*), Vice President Lyndon Johnson (*right*), and former Vice President Richard Nixon (*far right*).

could sit up front, but blacks had to sit in the back. Anderson insisted on "vertical seating" for her concerts, so that blacks would be able to buy seats in every part of the auditorium, and the best seats did not go only to whites. When Anderson traveled, she often was the only African American in the hotels where she stayed.

In 1939, Anderson wanted to sing at Constitution Hall in Washington, D.C. The Daughters of the American Revolution (DAR) would not allow African Americans to perform at the hall, which was their headquarters. First Lady Eleanor Roosevelt, who was a member of the organization, resigned over the decision. Roosevelt and Interior Secretary Harold Ickes arranged for Anderson to give a concert on the steps of the Lincoln Memorial instead. On Easter Sunday in 1939, Anderson sang "Ave Maria" and "America" to an audience of 75,000 people. A mural showing the event was painted on a wall in the Department of the Interior.

Anderson finally had her opportunity to perform at Constitution Hall

in 1942, when she gave a benefit concert for the U.S. Army Relief Fund.

Breaking More Barriers During the 1940s and the 1950s, Anderson continued to maintain a busy concert schedule. Her performances included many types of music. She sang traditional Negro spirituals as well as art songs and operatic arias written by classical composers.

On January 7, 1955, at the Metropolitan Opera House in New York City, Anderson sang the role of Ulrica, a fortune teller in the opera *Un Ballo in Maschera* (A Masked Ball) by the Italian composer Giuseppe Verdi. She was the first African American soloist in the history of the "Met." Her performance made the front page of the *New York Times*. Poet Langston Hughes called it "a precedent-shattering moment in American musical history." Anderson was 57 at the time.

Grateful for the opportunities she had received, Marian Anderson helped other young people pursue artistic careers.

A Remarkable Career

Anderson sang at the inaugural balls for Presidents Dwight D. Eisenhower and John F. Kennedy. In 1964, she performed a farewell tour that began at Constitution Hall and ended six months later at Carnegie Hall. Afterward, she lived in retirement on her farm in Connecticut with her husband, architect Orpheus Hodge Fisher.

Anderson won many awards in her lifetime, including

- the Spingarn Medal, given by the National Association for the Advancement of Colored People (NAACP);
- the Presidential Medal of Freedom;
- the Congressional Gold Medal.

The Bok Award, a $10,000 prize given to Anderson as an outstanding Philadelphia citizen, enabled her to establish the Marian Anderson Award to help young people of any race pursue an artistic career. In 1978, she was one of the first five Americans honored at the Kennedy Center for the Performing Arts in Washington, D.C.

Marian Anderson died in 1993. She had broken the color barrier in entertainment before baseball player Jackie Robinson broke it in sports. Her career opened doors for African American opera stars such as Leontyne Price, Jessye Norman, and Kathleen Battle. Anderson will long be remembered as one of the 20th century's greatest singers.

Margaret Bourke-White

Through her photographs, she captured the human drama of the 20th century.

A Serious Shutterbug

The only child of one of the inventors of color film, Margaret Bourke-White showed an early interest in photography. She was already an accomplished photographer by the time she graduated from Cornell University in 1927. Money she earned from selling her photos helped pay her college tuition.

After graduating, Bourke-White moved to Cleveland, Ohio, to live with her widowed mother. Bourke-White continued to take pictures and won first prize in a contest at the Cleveland Museum of Art. The focus of her work at this time was on architecture. She photographed buildings from unusual angles, so that people would look at them in a different way.

From the beginning of her career, the daring and headstrong Bourke-White went to great lengths to get the picture she wanted. She once borrowed a camera to capture a spontaneous scene she witnessed on the street. Fascinated by industrial machinery, she wanted to photograph steel production at a nearby steel mill. At first, the company refused, saying that a woman would faint in the mill's extreme heat. But Bourke-White persisted, and the steel company gave in. When Henry R. Luce, the founder of *Time* magazine, saw Bourke-White's photos called "The Story of Steel," he immediately offered her a job.

Eye on the World

In 1929, Bourke-White moved to New York and became a photographer for Luce's newest magazine, *Fortune.* She was a perfectionist with excellent technical skills. Luce encouraged her to use her skills to record on film important events as they were taking place. Photography was becoming an important part of journalism.

About this time, Bourke-White met the writer Erskine Caldwell at a party. Caldwell was about to begin a project on the effects of the Great Depression in the Deep South, and Bourke-White asked to join him. At first, Caldwell did not think that Bourke-White could photograph people, because her usual subjects were objects and buildings. Eventually, however, he agreed.

This joint venture had three important results. In 1937, their book *You Have Seen Their Faces* was published. The experience also opened Bourke-White's eyes to pain and poverty, themes she would revisit often in her work. And finally, Bourke-White and Caldwell fell in love.

Life's Lens In 1936, Luce made Bourke-White one of the first photographers for *Life,* a new kind of magazine in which pictures were as important as words. Bourke-White traveled the world, photographing important people and events. Her

Margaret Bourke-White was one of the first women to work in the male-dominated field of photojournalism.

reputation was so great that President Franklin Roosevelt singled her out from the pool of photographers who covered Washington and gave her special access to him. Covering the Soviet Union before World War II, Bourke-White and Caldwell were the only foreign journalists allowed to remain in Moscow when the German army invaded.

Bourke-White often risked her personal safety in performing her work. She made headlines herself when she disappeared in a swamp for a day. She was taking pictures alone when her boat broke down. It took her a day to reach a radio to call for help.

War Correspondent When the United States entered World War II, Bourke-White wanted to go to the front. In the spring of 1942, she was the first woman that the U.S. War Department authorized as a war photographer.

After several months in London, Bourke-White was assigned to cover the campaign in Algiers, North Africa. Flying was considered too dangerous for a woman, so Bourke-White traveled by boat. When the ship that carried her was torpedoed, the photographer discarded everything in her survival kit except one can of food. She wanted to make room in the kit for her camera.

Next, Bourke-White wanted to fly on a bombing mission, another activity off-limits to women. But General Jimmy Doolittle said, "Well, you've been torpedoed, you might as well go through everything." The dramatic photographs that Bourke-White sent back encouraged Americans' devotion to the war effort.

At the end of the war, Bourke-White traveled to Germany. There she photographed thousands of prisoners being released from the Nazi concentration camps. Her pictures had the power to make viewers care about the prisoners' suffering, just as her pictures of young soldiers at the front had aroused support for the war.

A Life in Focus

After the war, Bourke-White continued to place herself and her camera in the middle of the action, no matter where it was occurring. She traveled to India to capture images from the Pakistani war for independence. She photographed the Korean War from a bunker within 100 yards of enemy snipers. She recorded conditions for blacks in South Africa under the government's harsh apartheid policies.

While on assignment in Asia in 1954, Bourke-White noticed that she was having trouble walking. She had developed Parkinson's disease, a disorder of the nervous system that causes uncontrollable shaking. Eventually, it put an end to her career as a war correspondent. Still, she was able to write several books, including an autobiography titled *Portrait of Myself,* published in 1963. She died in 1971.

Margaret Bourke-White helped pioneer the field of photojournalism, telling stories through photographs rather than words. Today, her photos can be seen in the Library of Congress, the Brooklyn Museum, and the Museum of Modern Art in New York City. Her work influenced many other photographers, particularly during the Korean and Vietnam wars. Her photographs also changed the way that newspapers and magazines portray the world.

Bourke-White was in Germany when U.S. troops liberated the Nazi concentration camps. Her pictures and words captured the horror of what she saw there.

"Using the camera was almost a relief. It [placed] a slight barrier between myself and the horror in front of me."

—On photographing Buchenwald camp

Rachel Carson

A pioneer ecologist and popular science writer, she was a major force behind steps to protect the environment.

> *"The 'control of nature' is a phrase conceived in arrogance...when it was supposed that nature exists for the convenience of man....It is our alarming misfortune that [entomology—the study of insects] has armed itself with the most modern and terrible weapons, and that in turning them against the insects it has also turned them against the earth."*
>
> —From *Silent Spring*

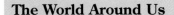

Carson suggested that carelessness with technology would destroy our earth.

Author and Animal Lover

Born in 1907, Rachel Louise Carson grew up surrounded by animals on 65 rural acres. The family owned a cow, chickens, rabbits, and pigs. If her mother found a spider in the house, she would take it outside and set it free rather than kill it. Rachel had a special fondness for cats and birds.

Rachel Carson showed an early talent for writing. When she was only nine years old, *St. Nicholas* magazine published her first story in its special section for young authors. The following year, the magazine published two more of Carson's stories.

In 1925, Carson received a scholarship to Pennsylvania College for Women (now Chatham College) in Pittsburgh. There she studied science and worked on the student newspaper and the literary magazine. When she received a fellowship to spend the summer at the Woods Hole Oceanographic Institute in Massachusetts, she saw the ocean for the first time. Carson followed her mother's respect for life as a model in her own work. After studying live creatures, Carson always returned them to their proper place in the sea.

The World Around Us

In 1935, Carson's father died. To support herself and her mother, Carson went to work for the U.S. Bureau of Fisheries, first as a writer and then as an aquatic biologist. During this time, she started writing articles about biology for the Baltimore *Sunday Sun.* Over the next ten years, she wrote for *Atlantic Monthly, Collier's, Field and Stream,* and other popular magazines. She also published her first book, *Under the Sea Wind.* In these writings, Carson explained that all living things and environments are related.

An Important Book In 1951, Carson published *The Sea Around Us.* In it, she described to the nonscientific reader the wonders of the ocean and its unusual creatures. As part of her research, she had gone deep-sea diving and spent ten days on a fishing boat. The book was a tremendous success both in the United States and abroad—it appeared on the bestseller list for 80 weeks and was translated into 32 languages.

Following the publication of *Silent Spring,* Rachel Carson testified in Congress. She urged lawmakers to restrict the sale of chemical pesticides and to stop aerial spraying.

The Sea Around Us was named "Outstanding Book of the Year" by the *New York Times* and won the National Book Award, the John Burroughs Medal for a natural history book of outstanding literary quality, and numerous science writing awards. The book also earned Carson honorary degrees from several colleges and universities. In 1953, it was made into an Academy Award–winning documentary film. The success generated by *The Sea Around Us* allowed Carson to leave her government job and concentrate on her own research and writing.

Beyond the Sea Rachel Carson would create an even greater stir with another book. During the 20th century, and particularly since the 1940s, the use of chemical pesticides in the United States had increased dramatically. Pesticides are agents that kill unwanted insects and weeds. New pesticides had vastly increased agricultural output and provided other benefits. In the 1950s, few people considered that they could also be dangerous.

Carson began to wonder about pesticides after receiving a letter from a friend who owned a private bird sanctuary near Boston. The friend told her that many birds had died very painfully after the area had been sprayed with DDT, a powerful pesticide that was used to kill mosquitoes and other insects. The friend asked if Carson knew anyone in Washington, D.C., who could help stop the spraying.

Carson started to investigate pesticides herself. When a citizens' group on Long Island, New York, sued the government to stop DDT spraying, Carson covered the trial as part of her research. She also corresponded with experts from around the world. She found that the potential problems with pesticides were worse than anyone had realized. She also saw that no one wanted to make the concerns public.

Carson presented her findings in *Silent Spring,* which was published in 1962. In it, she provided strong evidence that pesticide use was not just killing the pests but harming other wildlife as well. Carson wrote that when birds were exposed to DDT, their eggshells became thin, and their offspring could not survive. She further contended that pesticides pass through the food chain—as larger organisms consume smaller ones. As a result, the toxic chemicals could build up in the bodies of larger animals, including humans. Carson warned that unless people used chemicals more wisely, they risked doing great harm to the earth and its inhabitants.

Her Message Was Heard

Many chemical companies were threatened by Carson's conclusions. One company tried unsuccessfully to prevent her from publishing the book. Critics attacked her personally and professionally, trying to weaken her message. But enough people heard it, and they found the questions she raised troubling.

By the end of 1962, Washington was flooded with letters calling for further research into and control of pesticides. In response, the U.S. Congress enacted several laws regulating pesticide use and testing. Carson's contribution to these reforms was honored by such groups as the Animal Welfare Institute and the National Wildlife Federation. The following year, the President's Science Advisory Committee confirmed many of the points that Carson had brought to light in *Silent Spring.* DDT was banned in the United States in 1972.

Rachel Carson died of cancer and heart disease in 1964. In 1970, Interior Secretary Walter J. Hickel dedicated the Rachel Carson National Wildlife Refuge in Maine, where Carson had lived. A decade later, President Jimmy Carter awarded Carson the Presidential Medal of Freedom, the highest civilian award in the United States. Her work had generated a new level of environmental awareness in the American public and helped spur the environmental-protection movement.

Students at the Rachel Carson Wildlife Refuge in Maine learn about living things and their environments.

Mother Teresa

She is known around the world for her work to relieve the suffering of the poor and the dying.

Called to Serve

Agnes Gonxha Bojaxhiu was born in 1910, the daughter of an Albanian builder and merchant. Her mother was a devout Catholic who often visited the sick and needy. Young Agnes joined the Sodality of the Blessed Virgin Mary, a church organization that served the poor. When she was a teenager, she became inspired by letters written to her church from missionaries in India. She decided then what she wanted to do with her life.

At age 18, Agnes Bojaxhiu entered the convent of the Sisters of Loreto, an Irish order of nuns with a mission in Calcutta, India. She chose Teresa as her religious name after St. Thérèse de Lisieux, a 19th-century French nun whose life and work reflected goodness and charity. Mother Teresa taught history and geography at the Loreto school in Calcutta for 20 years. The school was within sight of one of the city's worst slums.

On September 10, 1946, Mother Teresa was on a train to the town of Darjeeling when she received what she described as a "call within a call"—a message from God calling her to live among the desperately poor. Two years later, she obtained permission to leave her convent, study nursing, and establish a school in the slums.

Much of Mother Teresa's work has been with children—providing shelter and education for them.

More than 13 million people live in Calcutta. Many of them live on the street or in makeshift homes like this.

Poorest of the Poor

In 1950, Mother Teresa received approval from the Catholic Church to establish a new religious community, the Missionaries of Charity. The order started with 12 women, mostly former students from the Loreto school. Their uniform was a simple blue and white sari. The sari is the traditional dress of Indian women.

The nuns awoke at 4 A.M. to say prayers and begin a 16-hour workday. They owned nothing except a single change of clothing. They ate the same food as the poor people around them. They received no payment for their work, nor did they accept any gifts—not even a cup of tea. According to Mother Teresa, "To be able to love the poor and know the poor, we must be poor ourselves."

Death with Dignity In 1954, Mother Teresa established the *Nirmal Hriday* (Pure Heart) Home for the Dying in a dormitory building donated by the city of Calcutta. In the streets of this city, people lay dying of starvation and disease. Mother Teresa eased their suffering by giving them shelter, washing them, and feeding them. One man said to her, "All my life I have lived like an animal on the streets; now I am dying like an angel."

As word of Mother Teresa's work spread, people donated money. She used these funds to establish an orphanage, a home for the elderly, a workshop for the unemployed, and a shelter for women and children. Pope Paul VI gave Mother Teresa a limousine that he had been given by the people of the United States. She immediately auctioned it and used the money to help people with leprosy build a community in West Bengal. People with leprosy, a progressive disease that causes disfigurement and paralysis, were often treated as outcasts, because the disease was believed to be highly contagious. Mother Teresa's work helped bring about greater understanding of the disease and compassion for its victims.

Each summer, intense monsoon rains strike India. The rains often cause flooding of low-lying areas. When the monsoon rains struck Calcutta, this five-foot-tall woman waded through the mud to rescue those stranded in the slums.

Reaching Out By 1960, the Missionaries of Charity had spread their work throughout India, having established missions and programs in 24 cities outside Calcutta. In 1965, Mother Teresa received permission to expand outside India. She opened centers in Venezuela, Ceylon, Rome, Tanzania, and Cuba.

People throughout the world learned of Mother Teresa's mission. She was honored by the government of India and by the pope. In 1979, she received the Nobel Peace Prize. She accepted this great honor not for herself, but "in the name of the hungry, of the naked, of the homeless, . . . of those who feel unwanted, uncared for." She upheld her vow of poverty by declining to attend the traditional banquet for winners. She used the $25,000 prize money to build more facilities for the sick and the poor.

Greater Love

At age 72, Mother Teresa went to Lebanon with a message of peace from Pope John Paul II. Three years later, in 1985, she addressed the General Assembly of the United Nations on its 40th anniversary. That same year, she joined Cardinal Cooke, archbishop of New York, in opening the first church-sponsored AIDS hospice. (A hospice provides treatment and comfort to those who are dying.)

A heart attack forced Mother Teresa to retire in 1990. But the work she began continues. Today, the Missionaries of Charity includes 4,000 sisters of different nationalities who work in the 500 centers Mother Teresa established. The missions feed over half a million families and educate some 20,000 children in 100 countries worldwide.

St. Thérèse said that good comes from performing everyday tasks with joy. Likewise, Mother Teresa believes that "We can do no great things, only small things with great love." Through her work, Mother Teresa has influenced millions of lives by teaching the young, caring for the destitute, sheltering orphans and unwanted children, and treating the sick in clinics. She has inspired countless more.

WOMEN NOBEL PRIZE WINNERS

Name	Nationality	Year	Category
Marie Curie	Polish-French	1903	Physics
		1911	Chemistry
Baroness Bertha von Suttner	Austrian	1905	Peace
Selma Lagerlof	Swedish	1909	Literature
Jane Addams	American	1931	Peace
Dorothy C. Hodgkin	British	1964	Chemistry
Mairead Corrigan and Betty Williams	N. Irish	1976	Peace
Rosalyn S. Yalow	American	1977	Physiology/Medicine
Mother Teresa of Calcutta	Albanian-Indian	1979	Peace
Alva Myrdal	Swedish	1982	Peace
Barbara McClintock	American	1983	Physiology/Medicine
Rita Levi-Montalcini	Italian-American	1986	Physiology/Medicine
Nadine Gordimer	S. African	1991	Literature
Aung San Suu Kyi	Burmese	1991	Peace
Rigoberta Menchú	Guatemalan	1992	Peace
Toni Morrison	American	1993	Literature

Each year, Nobel prizes are awarded for outstanding achievements in physics, chemistry, physiology and medicine, peace, literature, and economics. Here is a list of some of the women who have received Nobel prizes.

Indira Gandhi

As India's prime minister, she helped lead social and economic reform.

Political Family

Indira Nehru was born in 1917 into a wealthy Indian family. At the time she was born, India was part of the British Empire. Indira's grandfather, Motalil Nehru, and her father, Jawaharlal Nehru, were both lawyers. They were also Indian nationalists—they believed that India should be independent from Great Britain. Motalil Nehru felt so strongly about this that he burned everything he owned that was made outside of India. Young Indira followed her grandfather's example by burning her own favorite European doll, although it broke her heart to throw it onto the fire.

When Indira was four years old, her father and her grandfather were arrested and tried for speaking out against British authority. Throughout much of Indira's youth, her father was in and out of jail for protesting British rule. As a teenager, Indira became active in politics and the independence movement. In 1942, she herself spent most of a year in jail. That year she also married Feroze Gandhi, a childhood friend and a fellow nationalist. (He was not related to Mohandas Gandhi, the leader of India's independence movement.)

A New Nation Forms India finally won independence in 1947, and Jawaharlal Nehru became prime minister. His main tasks were to unify a huge country of many language, religious, and ethnic groups and to improve the way of life for millions of poor Indian people. Nehru served as prime minister until his death in 1964. Indira Gandhi, whose mother had died in 1936, often accompanied her father in his travels. She went with him to meet heads of state around the world.

Meanwhile, Indira Gandhi also pursued her own political career. In 1959, she became chairperson of the ruling Congress Party. She helped reorganize the party and bring in new members. She appealed to women and young people especially to become involved in politics and social issues. She also sought to unify party members from India's many different states and peoples and to create alliances with other political groups. She left the party leadership after a year, devoting her energy to social causes and to assisting her aging father.

Leading a Young Nation

Indira Gandhi traveled frequently to meet with people around India, a practice she would continue for the rest of her life. When China attacked the Indian town of Bom Dila in November 1962, she donated all her gold jewelry to raise money for national defense.

Three years later, when fighting broke out between India and Pakistan over the contested province of Kashmir, Gandhi went to the battlefront. There, she headed relief efforts and encouraged her side.

Winning the Election The death of her father began a new phase in the life and career of Indira Gandhi. In 1964, she was elected to the Indian Parliament and became minister of information and broadcasting.

A year and a half later, in 1966, the prime minister who had succeeded Jawaharlal Nehru died. Congress Party leaders turned to the popular and well-known Indira Gandhi to take his place. She became prime minister—leader of a democracy of 500 million people—by a vote of 355 to 169 in Parliament. In her acceptance speech, she said, "No matter what our language, our religion, or state, we are one nation and one people." Her first priority was to find ways to feed the millions of starving people in her country.

Selfless Service But Gandhi, like her father, had a difficult job ahead of her. Within hours of her being sworn in, a bloody riot occurred in the southern state of Kerala. The harvest had failed, and people were fighting

Because she came from a long line of political activists, it is not surprising that Indira Gandhi chose the same career for herself.

over food. Gandhi arranged for emergency shipments of rice. Then she flew to Kerala and encouraged the people to eat more wheat and other grains instead of rice. Gandhi gave up her own rice—one of her favorite foods—to set an example.

Gandhi took actions to help fight hunger all over India. She set up a program to import grain and fertilizer and distributed nearly 14 tons of grain to the Indian people. She supported programs to teach better farming methods. Gandhi also established "fair price" shops so that the cost of rice would not rise and fall as it had in the past.

A War on Poverty In addition to hunger, India faced other problems. These included extreme poverty, unemployment, and illiteracy. Gandhi established the Social Welfare Board, a network of social service agencies, to address some of these issues. She was particularly concerned about how India's problems affected the welfare of the children.

Gandhi also sought to end ethnic tensions. When terrible riots broke out between two of India's religious groups—Sikhs and Hindus—Gandhi traveled to the site of the conflict. Her presence there helped to pacify the rival groups.

Time for the People Indira Gandhi was unusual among national leaders. She was directly involved with individuals. She set aside an hour each day to meet with the people who gathered outside her office. She brought new people with new ideas into her cabinet (advisors), and she tried to streamline India's vast system of government. Following a major victory in a war with Pakistan in 1971, Indira Gandhi seemed to be at the height of her power and popularity.

Indira Gandhi is shown here meeting with veterans and war widows who had come seeking her protection from police brutality.

Caught in Controversy

State of Emergency But things soon changed. Economic conditions grew worse. Then, in 1975, she was found guilty of violating election laws and was ordered by the court to step down. Instead, Gandhi took a drastic step—she declared emergency rule, taking personal control over the country and suspending the democratic process.

During the emergency rule, Gandhi enacted rigid policies, and people lost many of their freedoms. She postponed elections and jailed many of her political opponents. To curb overpopulation, she enforced a mandatory birth control program. Her popularity plunged. When elections finally took place in 1977, Gandhi lost.

The Final Days Gandhi won back her support and regained power in 1980. But her final years in office were also troubled. Her son Sanjay,

Although troubled by religious conflict and poverty, India remains the world's most populous democracy.

her chief advisor, died in a plane crash. Sikh nationalists in northwest India staged violent protests, and Gandhi sent troops to stop them. This trouble simmered until 1984. That year, a Sikh member of Gandhi's own security force assassinated her. Despite the difficulties of Indira Gandhi's last years, she will be remembered as the first female leader of the world's second most populous nation.

FACTS ABOUT INDIA

India's land area is about 1,269,346 square miles, nearly one-third the size of the United States and 13 times the size of Great Britain.

India's population is approximately 907,442,000—73 percent rural and 27 percent urban.

Hindi is India's official language; English is widely used in business and government. There are 13 regional languages and hundreds of local dialects.

About 83 percent of Indians are Hindus, and 11 percent are Muslims. Christians, Sikhs, Buddhists, and Jains make up the remaining 6 percent.

Katharine Meyer Graham

As head of the Washington Post Company, she is one of America's most influential business leaders.

Family Footsteps

The daughter of an author and a wealthy banker, Katharine Meyer grew up surrounded by famous writers and other cultural figures. Born in New York City in 1917, she was raised in Washington, D.C. She attended private schools and enjoyed working on the school newspaper. When Meyer was in high school, her father bought the *Washington Post* newspaper.

Meyer worked at the *Post* during summer breaks from college. After graduation from college, she spent a year as a reporter for the *San Francisco News,* then joined the *Post* staff. Her jobs in the editorial and circulation departments taught her much about the different areas of the newspaper business.

In 1940, Katharine Meyer married Philip L. Graham. In 1945, she set aside her newspaper career to raise a family. While her husband built a publishing empire that included the *Post,* the *Washington Times-Herald, Newsweek* magazine, radio and television stations, and an international news service, she stayed home to raise their four children. Philip Graham died in 1963.

In this 1964 photo, Katharine Graham poses with a copy of the *Washington Post,* one of the world's most prestigious newspapers.

Taking the Helm

In September 1963, Katharine Graham switched from housewife and mother to president of the Washington Post Company. One of her first goals was to bring the paper to national prominence. To do so, she studied the paper's operation carefully, attending editorial meetings and interviewing reporters. She also sought advice from many well-known figures in Washington politics.

Katharine Graham increased the *Post*'s editorial budget in order to attract talented reporters and editors. She hired Benjamin Bradlee from *Newsweek*'s Washington bureau to edit the paper and gave him a free hand to choose the stories that he thought were most interesting and important. She did not insist that her publications follow any particular editorial policy, as some publishers do. She believed that editorial freedom would result in better journalism. With her contacts in Washington, Graham herself often was a good source of news tips.

Graham's approach worked. By 1966, the *Post* ranked third in the nation in advertising sales—a sign of a newspaper's business success. By 1970, more than half a million people read the daily *Post,* and 650,000 read the Sunday edition.

Pentagon Papers In 1971, Graham decided to sell public stock in the company, a move that would allow continued growth. At the same time, the *Post* was involved in an important event. The paper obtained some of the "Pentagon Papers"—documents from a secret Defense Department study of U.S. military involvement in Vietnam. They showed that government officials had misled the American people about the war. If the *Post* ran the story, the government could

In 1991, Donald Graham (*left*) became chief executive officer of the Washington Post Company. Executive editor Ben Bradlee looks on as the announcement is made.

sue the company. That would put an end to the stock sale. Such a lawsuit also would put the company's control of TV stations at risk. But Graham believed that the truth was more important. She gave her editors permission to run excerpts from the documents.

President Nixon ordered the newspapers to stop printing the Pentagon Papers. He claimed that their publication was endangering national security (the Vietnam War was still being fought). The issue went to the Supreme Court, which ruled that the newspapers had the right to run the story. The decision was considered a major victory for freedom of the press.

The Watergate Affair On Saturday, June 17, 1972, Graham received a call from the *Post*'s managing editor, as she did most Saturdays. The editor ran down the stories for Sunday's paper, including one about a suspicious break-in at the Watergate office building in Washington. A group of five men had burglarized Democratic Party headquarters—in the middle of a presidential election year. The next day, the *Post* ran the Watergate break-in story on the front page. But no one knew then how far the story would eventually lead.

Robert Woodward and Carl Bernstein, two young *Post* reporters, followed the story for months as they uncovered new information about who was behind the break-in. It soon became apparent that the affair involved the staff of President Nixon's reelection campaign.

It also became clear that the administration was trying to cover its tracks. Secretary of State Henry Kissinger warned her that the paper was taking a big political risk by pursuing the story. John Mitchell, who had been Nixon's attorney general, made outright threats. But Graham had faith in her editors and reporters and did not back down.

Finally, the *Post* team traced the Watergate cover-up all the way to the White House. Their work earned the *Post* a Pulitzer Prize, journalism's top award. The stories also made the *Washington Post* world famous.

Running a large corporation has traditionally been men's work. These days, an increasing number of women are joining the executive ranks. Here is a list of some of them and the corporations they run.

Leaving a Legacy

In 1979, Graham began to turn over some of her duties to her oldest son, Donald. She still heads the executive committee of the Washington Post Company's board of directors.

Today, the *Washington Post* is one of the most influential papers in the United States. It is read by officials and employees of almost all federal government agencies and diplomatic staffs around the world. The Washington Post Company is now a huge communication empire. Its *Newsweek* magazine is the second largest American newsweekly. In addition to the paper and the magazine, the company's holdings include

- several television stations and cable television systems.
- the Stanley H. Kaplan Educational Center, a test preparation company.
- an on-line information service about federal legislation.

Katharine Meyer Graham oversees it all in the family tradition of intellectual freedom, free speech, public service, and good business sense. Her success has made her one of the most influential women in America.

EXECUTIVE WOMEN

Name	Title	Company
Jill Barad	President	Mattel USA
Brenda Barnes	President	Pepsi-Cola South
Ellen R. Gordon	President	Tootsie Roll Industries
Helene Hahn	Executive Vice President	Disney Studios
Ellen M. Hancock	Vice President and General Manager	IBM
Katherine M. Hudson	Vice President	Eastman Kodak
Lois Juliber	Chief Technological Officer	Colgate-Palmolive
Kay Koplovitz	Chief Executive Officer	USA Network
Ellen R. Marram	President	RJR Nabisco
Carole A. Presley	Senior Vice President	Federal Express

Maya Angelou

This multitalented writer has inspired millions with her poetry and autobiographical books.

In the early 1960s, Maya Angelou began to use her creative talents to campaign for the civil rights of African Americans.

Pain and Poetry

Marguerite Johnson was born on April 4, 1928, in St. Louis, Missouri. When she was three, her parents divorced. Johnson spent her childhood being shuttled between her father, her mother, and her grandmother, who ran a general store in rural Arkansas.

At age eight, Marguerite Johnson was abused by her mother's boyfriend. She stopped speaking for five years, until a family friend introduced her to poetry and philosophy. Johnson began writing poetry of her own and graduated from eighth grade at the top of her class. In high school, she studied drama and dance. But her troubles had not ended.

In response to an interviewer's question, Angelou suggested that, even after times of pain and struggle, each new day brings renewed hope.

At age 15, Johnson ran away from her father's house after a quarrel with his girlfriend. For a month she lived in an abandoned van. She dropped out of school and, at age 16, had a son.

For the next several years, Johnson drifted between California and Arkansas. She held odd jobs—cook, streetcar attendant, and waitress. A break came when she was hired to dance in a bar.

The Caged Bird Soars

The new job meant a new beginning. Marguerite Johnson took a new name as well. "Maya" was her brother's nickname for her; "Angelou" came from Angelos, the name of the man to whom she had been married for a short time. Dancing in fancy night-clubs opened up new opportunities. In the mid-1950s, Angelou toured Africa and Europe in the show *Porgy and Bess*. Working as a professional dancer in the show helped build her self-confidence.

Art for Change's Sake While working as a performer, Angelou put her creative gifts to use for the civil rights movement and other social causes. With comedian Godfrey Cambridge, she cowrote a show called *Cabaret for Freedom* to benefit Martin Luther King Jr.'s Southern Christian Leadership Conference. Angelou worked for King's organization in the early 1960s.

By the time Angelou was 30, she had decided that she wanted to be a poet. She attended weekly meetings of the Harlem Writer's Guild. There she met the author James Baldwin and other important African American writers. Some of Angelou's friends encouraged her to write the story of her interesting, and often painful, life. Angelou dedicated

"There is that in the human breast, that despite nights of terror, and fear, and pain, and grief, and disconsolation, somehow morning comes and we get up and continue on."
—*Ebony*, April 1993

herself to writing, but she would have many more experiences before her life story became literature.

In late 1961, Angelou moved to Egypt, where she worked as an editor for the *Arab Observer,* an English-language newsweekly. Angelou decided to visit Ghana to learn more about her African ancestry. Although life was very different in Ghana, in some ways it reminded Angelou of her girlhood. She later wrote: "The erect and graceful walk of the women reminded me of my Arkansas Grandmother, Sunday-hatted, on her way to church. I listened to men talk, and whether or not I understood their meaning, there was a melody as familiar as sweet potato pie. . . ."

Angelou stayed in Ghana for several years, working as a writer and editor and teaching at the University of Ghana. Although Angelou felt very much at home in Africa, she felt that Africans considered her an outsider, an American. She returned to the United States in 1966. While she wrote many poems, stories, scripts, and songs, ideas for a major book began to take shape.

First Life Story In 1970, Angelou published *I Know Why the Caged Bird Sings,* an autobiography of her childhood in Arkansas. Written with great humor, warmth, and wisdom, it recounts Angelou's childhood abuse and five-year silence and ends with the birth of her son, Guy. The book was praised by critics and embraced by the public, which made it a bestseller. In 1979, Angelou wrote the script and music for a television version of the book.

I Know Why the Caged Bird Sings was the first of several books in which Angelou shares her life story. The sequels include *Gather Together in My Name, All God's Children Need*

Once people knew that Angelou had been asked to write the inaugural poem, they would stop her and ask if she had finished writing it yet.

Traveling Shoes, and *The Heart of a Woman.* With these books, Angelou moved to the forefront of American authors.

In 1972, Angelou became the first African American woman to have a screenplay produced by Hollywood. The movie was called *Georgia, Georgia.* Meanwhile, Angelou continued to act occasionally, performing on Broadway and on television. Her work in the TV miniseries of Alex Haley's *Roots* earned her an Emmy nomination.

But poetry was still Angelou's first love. She wrote several books of poems about society and about being black. They include *Oh Pray My Wings Are Gonna Fit Me Well* and *I Shall Not Be Moved.* In 1981, Angelou received a lifetime appointment as Reynolds Professor of American Studies at Wake Forest University in North Carolina.

Still Singing

Maya Angelou's writings are more popular now than ever. Sales of her books skyrocketed after Bill Clinton asked her to write a poem for his 1993 presidential inauguration. On January 20, 1993, Angelou read *On the Pulse of Morning* and won the hearts of Americans across the nation.

This vital and creative woman is still at work. In 1993, she directed *And Still I Rise,* the stage version of one of her poems, and hosted *Maya Angelou's America: A Journey of the Heart* on public television. She is a popular speaker, spreading her message that people are more alike than they are different and that their differences should be celebrated, not feared.

Although Maya Angelou writes about the African American experience, her books also are about the journey that each person makes through life, growing emotionally and spiritually. Somehow, says Angelou, people find strength despite hardships.

Violeta Chamorro

As president of Nicaragua, she ushered in a new era of democracy in her country.

Country in Turmoil

Nicaragua gained independence from Spain in 1821. Since then, the political history of this Central American nation had been marked by a series of revolutions. The power struggles came to an end in 1936, when General Anastasio Somoza seized command of the country. The Somoza family ruled for more than 40 years. During their regime, government corruption was common. Political dissent was not tolerated.

La Prensa In 1929, Violeta Barrios was born into a wealthy Nicaraguan family. Her family sent her to high school in the United States. After returning to Nicaragua, she met the man who would change the course of her life. Pedro Joaquín Chamorro was editor and publisher of a newspaper called *La Prensa* (The Press) and a strong opponent of General Somoza. Violeta Barrios and Pedro Chamorro married in 1950.

After Pedro Chamorro was fatally shot in 1978, Violeta Chamorro took over the operation of *La Prensa*. She began a campaign of support for the guerrillas of the Sandinista National Liberation Front (FSLN), who wanted to overthrow the Somoza regime.

From Bad to Worse In 1979, the Sandinistas succeeded in ousting the Somozas. But life in Nicaragua improved very little. Faced with serious economic problems, the Sandinistas attempted to bring about sweeping changes in the country. They took control of privately owned lands and industries. They also strengthened the military while the nation's economy worsened.

The Making of a President

The Sandinistas gave Violeta Chamorro a position in the new government. They did this, in part, because of her support during the fight against the Somozas. But they also wanted the power and influence of *La Prensa* behind them, and they valued Chamorro's connections to Nicaragua's wealthy families. Chamorro took the post because "it would be unpatriotic to refuse." However, less than a year later, she resigned. She believed that the Sandinista regime had become as rigid as the one that it had overthrown. For example, it did not allow citizens to protest government policies or allow workers to strike for better conditions. Chamorro saw that the regime was unwilling to support a democracy in Nicaragua.

Civil War Meanwhile, groups of anti-Sandinista rebels known as contras (from the Spanish word for "against") were organizing with support from the U.S. government. In the early 1980s, a civil war began between the Sandinista government and the contras.

Chamorro and *La Prensa* sided with the contras. The Sandinistas reacted by censoring *La Prensa* and attempting to take control of the newspaper. In 1986, they forced Chamorro to stop publishing and threatened her safety. She was even accused of treason. After the paper had been shut down for 15 months, the government allowed it to reopen. Meanwhile, the civil war turmoil continued.

Other Central American countries were concerned about events in

Violeta Chamorro is shown here in her well-known white suit acknowledging the applause of her supporters.

A worker at *La Prensa* stacks copies of the newspaper announcing Chamorro's election victory.

Nicaragua. The leaders of these countries pressured the Sandinistas to hold democratic elections. They agreed to do so if the contras would disband. An agreement was reached, and elections were scheduled.

Leading an Opposition In September 1989, Chamorro was nominated to run for president. Her support came from 14 anti-Sandinista groups that had joined together to form the National Opposition Union. The union represented a wide range of political philosophies, from conservative to Communist. What they had in common was a belief that Violeta Chamorro could unite the country. Even though she had had little experience in politics, she was a familiar and respected figure among the people of Nicaragua.

Chamorro campaigned vigorously throughout the country. She often appeared dressed in white, traveling in a white wagon. She sought the support of the average Nicaraguan citizen. Her goal was to build a strong national economy. She also called for an end to the violence and political repression that Nicaraguans had endured under the Somoza regime and then under the Sandinistas.

Victory Voting occurred on February 25, 1990. It was probably the most closely watched election in the history of Central America. Before the election, polls had given the lead to President Daniel Ortega Saavedra, the Sandinista leader. But when the official ballots were counted, Violeta Chamorro had won the presidency by a 15 percent margin. Her supporters, the National Opposition Union, won 52 out of the 91 seats in the National Assembly.

Chamorro took office in April 1990. As she had promised during her campaign, the new president granted amnesty both to Sandinistas and contras. Pleased with the outcome of the election, the U.S. government lifted the trade embargo (a restriction on commerce) it had imposed against Nicaragua in 1985.

Solutions and Problems

One of Chamorro's most significant achievements as president was in persuading more than 22,000 contra rebels to abandon their jungle camps and turn over their weapons to the United Nations. In return, the contras received land and food. The agreement ended a civil war that had cost at least 30,000 lives.

Woman in the Middle Chamorro's presidency has not been easy. She faces extremely high inflation, and two-thirds of the Nicaraguan people are unemployed. Although she led the country out of civil war, bitter political divisions still exist. Many people disapprove of Chamorro's inclusion of Sandinistas in her government. But the Sandinistas are still the largest single party in the country, and she wants them on her side.

Violeta Chamorro's independent thinking has placed her in the middle of a heated debate. Her own family is divided over her policies. Despite the continuing turmoil around her, Violeta Chamorro is recognized and honored the world over for her struggle to unite her people and preserve freedom of expression in Nicaragua.

Events in Nicaraguan History

1821	Nicaragua and other Central American countries declare independence from Spain and establish the Mexican Empire.
1838	Nicaragua becomes a separate republic; civil war begins.
1936	General Anastasio Somoza seizes power.
1950	Violeta Barrios marries Joaquin Chamorro, opposition leader and newspaper publisher.
1956	Anastasio Somoza is assassinated (and succeeded by his sons Luis in 1957 and Anastasio in 1972).
1978	Joaquin Chamorro is assassinated.
1979	Sandinista guerrillas overthrow the Somoza regime.
1984	Daniel Ortega wins presidential election and establishes close ties with Cuba and other Communist countries.
	With U.S. support, contras begin guerrilla warfare against the Sandinistas.
1989	Pressure for democratic reforms results in free elections.
1990	Violeta Chamorro succeeds Ortega as president.

Jane Goodall

Her extensive research on chimpanzees in the wild led to a new way of studying animals.

In this photo, Goodall and a chimpanzee observe each other. In this way, the chimps came to trust her.

Interest in Animals

Jane Goodall was only 18 months old when she met her first chimpanzee. The chimp, named Jubilee, was a toy that her mother had given her. The stuffed animal was made in honor of the first chimpanzee born in captivity at the London Zoo. Goodall always kept Jubilee with her, even after she started working with live chimpanzees in Africa.

Goodall was born in England in 1934. Even as a little girl, she loved animals. She once watched a hen for hours until it laid an egg. She was enchanted with the stories of Dr. Dolittle, the fictional English doctor who "talked to the animals." After reading *Tarzan* and *The Jungle Book,* she decided to study animals in Africa when she grew up.

As an adult, Goodall moved to east Africa, where she met Louis Leakey, a famous anthropologist. Leakey thought that the best way to learn more about early humans would be to observe other primates in the wild. Primates is the classification of mammals that includes apes and monkeys as well as humans. Leakey arranged for Goodall to study chimpanzees.

In Africa

Seeing the Differences In 1960, Jane Goodall arrived at the Gombe Stream Reserve on Lake Tanganyika in Tanzania, accompanied by her mother, a game ranger, and a cook. Researchers had come there before Goodall, but none had ever been able to get close to the chimps. Jane Goodall was different. She was not afraid to go out into the jungle alone, and gradually the chimps became curious about her. At first, all the chimps looked alike to her. Soon, Goodall began to notice distinguishing characteristics. She gave them names based on their appearance or personality—Flo, David Graybeard, Olly, Passion, and others.

Jane Goodall observed aspects of chimpanzee behavior that earlier researchers had not. For example, some researchers saw the chimps as violent animals, but Goodall saw their gentleness. She observed them holding hands, grooming one another's hair and skin, and kissing one another in greeting. In order to get a closer look at the world from a chimp's-eye view, Goodall imitated their behavior. She crouched on the ground as they did and ate the food they ate—even termites.

Goodall discovered that, contrary to what scientists had believed, chimps hunted, ate meat, and used tools. She noticed, for example, that the chimpanzees used sticks to dig termites out of the ground. This was a startling discovery, for it had been thought that humans were the only animals to make and use tools.

The map shows the location of Gombe where Goodall first began her animal behavior studies.

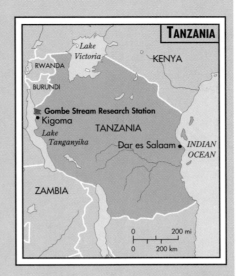

Names or Numbers? After about 18 months of study, Goodall presented her findings. At the time, most other animal behaviorists were male. Many of them criticized Goodall for naming her subjects instead of giving them numbers. Her critics accused her work of being overly influenced by emotion and opinion rather than being strictly based on measurements and statistics. Some of her critics may have been jealous of the attention that Goodall's research received in *National Geographic* magazine.

When Goodall returned to her work, she did something else that no other animal behaviorist ever had—she began to interact with the chimps. She started by offering them bananas. Eventually, they began to approach her. Finally, on Christmas Day in 1962, the chimp that Goodall had named David Graybeard allowed her to groom him for a full minute.

In 1967, when a polio epidemic hit the chimps, Goodall obtained medication for the afflicted chimpanzees. Some people criticized her for not letting nature take its course. But Goodall felt an obligation to ease the pain of the suffering chimps whom she had come to know so well.

Natural Child Rearing In 1964, Jane Goodall married Baron Hugo van Lawick, a Dutch photographer who had been filming her work. When their son was born in 1967, Goodall adopted many of the same child-rearing techniques that she had observed among the chimps. One chimp in particular, Flo, seemed to raise the most confident, socially skilled offspring. Goodall followed Flo's example. She breast-fed the baby, cradled him, and always kept him with her. On speaking tours, Goodall stressed the importance of the early mother-child relationship. She promoted the value of the traditional woman's role as mother. Her beliefs made her unpopular with some feminists, but they also gave many young mothers the encouragement they needed to stay home with their children.

Goodall and an assistant tend orphan chimpanzees while awaiting the construction of a new refuge.

After Africa

Goodall took her own advice. After her son was born, she spent less time at Gombe. As a visiting professor at Stanford University, she was able to recruit students to help with her fieldwork. She also took time to write a book, *In the Shadow of Man.* In 1980, the research station was opened to tourists.

Goodall spends several weeks each year at Gombe. Much of her time is spent visiting laboratories and zoos and advocating better conditions for captive animals, especially primates. The Jane Goodall Institute was established in 1977 to carry out this work.

Between 1962 and 1989, the National Geographic Society made five films about Goodall's work. Goodall proved that chimpanzees are much more like humans than anyone expected. Today, genetic studies show that chimps are closer to human beings than they are to the other apes. Many experts consider Goodall's research to be among the most important animal behavior studies in history. Her methods are now held as an example of how animal field studies should be done.

Barbara Jordan

The first African American woman ever elected to Congress from the South, she became a distinguished political and legal scholar.

Barbara Jordan gained national prominence during the hearings on the Watergate break-in and cover-up.

Building a Platform

The daughter of a Baptist minister, Barbara Jordan was born in 1936. She grew up in Houston, Texas, where she was a "straight-A" student. After hearing an African American woman attorney speak at a high school career day, Jordan decided to become a lawyer.

To prepare for her chosen career, Jordan competed successfully in local and national public speaking contests. At Texas Southern University, Jordan 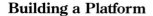studied political science and history and led the championship debate team.

Jordan was the first African American student at Boston University Law School. After earning her law degree, she went to work for a judge and became involved in Democratic Party politics. She organized African Americans to vote for John F. Kennedy and Lyndon Johnson in the 1960 presidential election. She herself ran unsuccessfully for the Texas House of Representatives in 1962 and 1964.

In 1966, Jordan won her first election—to the Texas State Senate. She was the first woman ever elected to this body and the first African American since 1883. In the Texas senate, Jordan sponsored civil rights legislation and laws that addressed urban problems, called for a minimum working wage, and proposed pollution controls. Jordan's effectiveness in the Texas senate caught the attention of President Lyndon Johnson. A fellow Texan, he invited Jordan to Washington, D.C., to consult her about federal civil rights legislation.

> "She proved that black is beautiful before we knew what it meant. She is involved in a governmental system of all the people, all the races, all economic groups."
>
> —**President Lyndon B. Johnson**

As an able lawmaker and a well-respected member of Congress, Barbara Jordan was publicly praised by President Lyndon Johnson.

National Affairs

Jordan was so successful in the Texas senate that in 1968 she ran for reelection unopposed. She also set her sights higher—on Washington, D.C. In 1971, Jordan announced her intention to run for the U.S. House of Representatives in the newly created 18th Congressional District in Texas. In the Democratic primary, Jordan received 80 percent of the vote, even though she was one of four candidates. In the regular election, Jordan defeated her Republican opponent just as easily. In January 1973, she began the first of three terms in Congress.

For the Record Jordan was a conscientious representative. During her first year in office, she never missed a vote. Although some black leaders wanted her to become a spokesperson for civil rights, she did not want to limit herself to a single issue. She believed very strongly that she had been elected to serve all her constituents and all Americans.

Jordan was soon recognized as a leading liberal voice in the Democratic Party. She supported legislation to aid the poor, the elderly, and women. She backed consumer- and environmental-protection laws. She voted to increase federal spending on schools and health programs. She favored ending the war in Vietnam and reducing federal spending on the military.

In the Limelight At the time Barbara Jordan entered Congress, a major scandal was developing in the White House. During the 1972 campaign, in which Republican President Richard Nixon was reelected, a break-in had occurred at the Democratic Party headquarters. The headquarters were in the Watergate office building in Washington. In 1973, televised hearings in the U.S. Senate uncovered much evidence that Nixon's closest aides—and perhaps the President himself—were involved in illegal activity related to the break-in.

Barbara Jordan was on the House Judiciary Committee, which investigates legal issues. In 1974, the committee decided to expand its investigation by holding hearings to determine whether there was enough evidence to impeach Nixon for his role in the Watergate scandal. If impeached, the President would be tried by the Senate. If found guilty, he would be removed from office.

To Impeach or Not to Impeach Jordan approached the complex issues carefully. She personally did not want to see a President impeached. But she felt that the evidence that Nixon helped cover up illegal activity demanded that he be brought to trial. She said that the President has a duty to uphold the Constitution. She contended that, in neglecting this duty, Nixon weakened the American system of government. During the televised hearings, a news correspondent called Jordan "the best mind on the committee" because of her legal knowledge and eloquence.

On July 30, 1974, the committee voted to impeach Nixon for obstructing investigations and abusing his presidential powers. Richard Nixon resigned from office on August 9.

The Keynote of a Career

In 1976, Barbara Jordan became the first African American keynote speaker at a national party convention. (The keynote speaker gives a major speech to open the convention.) In her stirring address, she expressed her belief that American democracy is the best in the world—but there are ways to make it work better for Americans. "We cannot improve on the system of government handed down to us by the founders of the Republic," she said, "but we can find new ways to implement that system and realize our destiny."

Private Citizen Shortly afterward, in 1979, Jordan found a new way to serve. She left politics for education, becoming a distinguished professor at the University of Texas School of Public Affairs. In addition to teaching, she has served as a recruiter of minority students for the school. For ten years, she also hosted a public affairs program, "Crisis to Crisis with Barbara Jordan," on public television.

Jordan has received more than 20 honorary doctoral degrees. Her honors include the Eleanor Roosevelt Humanities Award and election to a place in the Texas Women's Hall of Fame. In 1991, Texas governor Ann Richards named Jordan special counsel on government ethics.

Throughout her life, Barbara Jordan has worked to make government more ethical, more diverse, and more effective. Like the attorney who first inspired her, Barbara Jordan is a role model for women and minorities who wish to enter law and politics.

After her keynote address at the 1992 Democratic national convention, Barbara Jordan received a standing ovation.

Aung San Suu Kyi

A human rights activist, she is the leader of Burma's democracy movement and a political prisoner in her homeland.

Independence and Strife

Burma Days Aung San Suu Kyi's story begins with her father, Aung San, and the fight for Burmese independence. Aung San is a national hero, as George Washington is in the United States. From the 13th to the 20th centuries, the Southeast Asian nation of Burma had been under foreign rule. In the early 20th century, Burma was ruled by Great Britain and was considered part of India. A growing Burmese independence movement forced Britain to separate Burma from India in 1937. The Burmese people were allowed to elect representatives to a national assembly, but Great Britain appointed the governor.

Burmese nationalists continued to push for complete independence. One of their leaders was Aung San, who established an army to fight for this cause. World War II came, however, and Burma was taken over by Japan. Believing that Japan posed a greater obstacle to independence, Aung San led his army to fight with the British to defeat the Japanese.

In 1947, Great Britain finally agreed to Burmese independence. Elections were held, and a transitional government was established with Aung San as leader. He and his party laid the groundwork for a democracy in Burma. But before he could take office, he and several aides were assassinated by political rivals.

The following year, the nation achieved full independence from Great Britain. Aung San's daughter, Aung San Suu Kyi, was just three years old. One day, the little girl, whose name means "bright collection of strange victories," would play an important role in Burmese history herself.

Studying Abroad In 1960, Aung San's widow, Khin Kyi, was named ambassador to India. Suu Kyi went with her mother to live in New Delhi, the capital of India. At school there, Suu Kyi learned about Mohandas Gandhi's philosophy of nonviolent protest. She continued her education in England, where she studied politics, economics, and philosophy at Oxford University.

BURMA (MYANMAR)

★ National capital
• Other city

After graduating, Suu Kyi taught in England and worked at the United Nations in New York City. She also lived in Bhutan (northeast of India) and Japan before settling in England with her husband, Dr. Michael Aris, an Oxford professor. When Suu Kyi married Aris, she told him that someday she might have to return to her homeland to help her people.

Trouble at Home In 1962, while Suu Kyi was in England, General U Ne Win seized power from the civilian democratic government. A military dictator, Win ruled with an iron fist. He made sweeping changes to the economy, bringing industry and agriculture under government ownership and control. He used his military power to prevent people from opposing him. He also tried to isolate the nation politically from the rest of the world.

Win ruled Burma—which he officially renamed Myanmar—for more than 25 years. (Aung San Suu Kyi and her supporters have not accepted the new name.) In that time, the country suffered. No longer a major rice exporter as before, it became one of the world's poorest nations. In 1988, Win was forced to resign after university students and other people across the country protested his government. But Win continued to rule from behind the scenes. He appointed one of his military generals to take his place. The government set up a military junta, or council, called the State Law and Order Restoration Council, to silence those who protested too loudly. More than 3,000 Burmese who demonstrated against the junta and for democracy were massacred.

This map shows the location of Burma (Myanmar) in Southeast Asia.

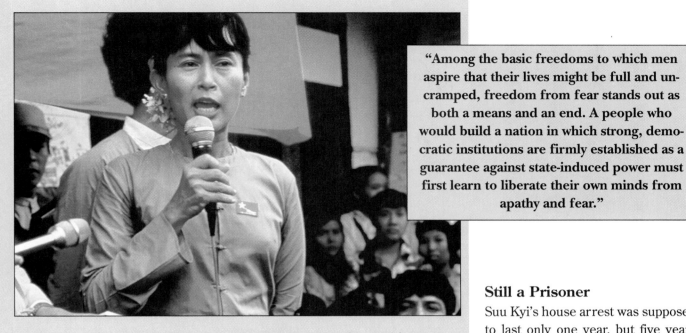

"Among the basic freedoms to which men aspire that their lives might be full and un-cramped, freedom from fear stands out as both a means and an end. A people who would build a nation in which strong, democratic institutions are firmly established as a guarantee against state-induced power must first learn to liberate their own minds from apathy and fear."

Aung San Suu Kyi is shown here giving one of her last public speeches before the government placed her under house arrest. In this quote, she echoes the words of former U.S. President Franklin Roosevelt in calling for the right of all people to live without fear of government tyranny.

The Spirit of Democracy

In April 1988, Aung San Suu Kyi returned to Burma to nurse her ailing mother. Suu Kyi found her homeland in chaos. As the daughter of a national hero, she felt a moral obligation to become involved in the pro-democracy struggle. She organized the protesters into the National League for Democracy (NLD) and served as its general secretary. The group called for a democratic government with representation from all regions and ethnic groups in Burma. Although the junta outlawed political gatherings, the NLD staged large, peaceful protests.

Suu Kyi believed strongly in Mohandas Gandhi's principles of nonviolent protest. She also possessed the courage of her father. Once Suu Kyi and her followers were confronted by armed soldiers on the street. She walked up to the soldiers alone, daring them to act. The soldiers backed down. Recalling the event later, she said, "It seemed so much simpler to provide them with a single target than to bring everyone else in."

Across Burma, more and more people joined in protests against the government. In an attempt to quell this tide, the junta finally agreed in 1989 to hold elections. The military leaders thought that they could control the outcome of the elections. When the junta saw the strong wave of public support for Aung San Suu Kyi, the council put her under house arrest. That was on July 20, 1989. Other NLD leaders were forced to leave the country.

Elections were held in May 1990, and Suu Kyi's NLD party won a huge victory—80 percent of the seats in the nation's legislature. But the generals refused to give up power. They also continued to arrest and imprison leaders of the NLD and other election winners.

Still a Prisoner

Suu Kyi's house arrest was supposed to last only one year, but five years later it continues. She is not allowed to leave her home in Rangoon. The telephone lines have been cut, and she is allowed few visitors. Even her husband and two sons, Kim and Alexander, are rarely permitted to see her.

In 1991, the military government asked Suu Kyi to leave the country and not return. She agreed to leave only if the junta agreed to turn over power to the people and release all political prisoners. The government refused. That year, Suu Kyi won the Nobel Peace Prize for her "nonviolent struggle for democracy and human rights." She learned of her award from a foreign radio broadcast. In 1992, the United Nations called for her release from arrest.

Two of Aung San Suu Kyi's heroes are Jawaharlal Nehru, India's first prime minister, and Nelson Mandela, the leader of South Africa's African National Congress. Both men spent much time in jail for their political convictions before accomplishing their goals. In Burma, where the people wear buttons with her picture, Suu Kyi is, like these leaders, a symbol of hope for freedom.

Wilma Mankiller

~~~~~~~~

As the first woman chief of the Cherokee Nation, she improved living conditions for Native Americans.

Trail of Tears

Once, the Cherokee Nation was the most powerful group in the region that is now North and South Carolina, Georgia, and Tennessee. After the arrival of the Europeans and the American War of Independence, the Cherokee way of life changed drastically. The Cherokee adopted many features of European culture. These included a constitutional government, agriculture, and even slavery. They also developed an alphabet so that they could read and write their language.

Other changes were forced upon the Cherokee Nation. In the 1830s, the U.S. government forced several treaties on the Cherokee to acquire their lands. The Native Americans received little in return or were offered false guarantees of other lands. As a result of one of these treaties, the Cherokee lost nearly 7 million acres and were forced to move to Indian Territory (now Oklahoma).

The march west came to be called the Trail of Tears, because about 4,000 of the 15,000 who began the journey died along the way. By the early 1900s, the federal government had taken away tribal ownership of their Oklahoma lands. Most Cherokee lived in extreme poverty.

Wilma Pearl Mankiller was born to a struggling Oklahoma family in 1945. Her mother was half Dutch, half Irish. Her father, Charley Mankiller, was a full-blooded Cherokee. His last name was a military title that had been in the family for generations.

A Woman and Her People

The Mankillers lived near Tahlequah, Oklahoma, on a 160-acre farm with no electricity or indoor plumbing. In the 1950s, drought caused the farm to fail, and the family moved to San Francisco. The city was a strange new world for the nine Mankiller children, who had never even seen an elevator before. Although she was a long way from Oklahoma, Wilma Mankiller never lost touch with her Native American heritage.

Alcatraz In the late 1960s, Wilma Mankiller was a young homemaker and mother, when something happened that would change the direction of her life. From November 1969 until June 1971, a group of Native Americans from different tribes took over abandoned prison buildings on Alcatraz Island in San Francisco Bay. The demonstrators' cause was called the American Indian Rights Movement. They hoped that their protest would call attention to the needs of their people—better education, better health care, and better living conditions. They also wanted the government to honor the past treaties that it had signed.

Mankiller agreed with the protesters and became interested in the idea of working to help Native Americans. She visited the demonstrators frequently and raised money to help their cause. Over the next few years, she took college courses and developed Native American programs for the Oakland, California, school system. Eventually, Mankiller moved

This contemporary painting shows the intense struggle of the Cherokee people as they were forced off their land and made to move to the Indian Territory of Oklahoma.

I want to be remembered as the person who helped us restore faith in ourselves."

—*Chicago Tribune* interview, May 14, 1986

After overcoming great personal misfortunes, Wilma Mankiller went on to become the leader of the Cherokee Nation.

back to Oklahoma, where she graduated from Flaming Rainbow University with a degree in social science.

Near Death Mankiller was working as community development director for the Cherokee Nation in 1979, when she was nearly killed in a head-on automobile collision. She broke both legs and many ribs, and part of her face was crushed. In the hospital she learned that she had myasthenia gravis, a nerve disease characterized by a progressive weakness in the muscles. Instead of feeling defeated by these setbacks, Mankiller later said that they helped make her strong enough to be a good leader.

After 17 operations, Mankiller recovered from the accident. She returned to her work for the government of the Cherokee Nation. She helped the town of Bell, Oklahoma, raise money to bring running water into the townspeople's homes for the first time. She raised money for better housing, too. Her activities caught the attention of Ross Swimmer, principal chief of the Cherokee Nation.

In 1983, Swimmer convinced Mankiller to run for deputy chief, a position comparable to vice president. In 1985, Swimmer went to Washington, D.C., to head the federal government's Bureau of Indian Affairs. Wilma Mankiller was then sworn in as the first woman principal chief of the Cherokee Nation.

Beloved Woman Mankiller's husband, Charley Soap, encouraged her to run for chief again in 1987. Some of the tribal elders were opposed to the idea, but Soap reminded them that long ago, before the Europeans arrived on the continent, Cherokee women had played important leadership roles. Women helped choose tribal leaders, and particularly important Cherokee women received the title "Beloved Woman." The elders were persuaded.

Even though Wilma Mankiller ran against three men in that election, she received 46 percent of the vote. A runoff election was held, and Mankiller won by a solid majority. She was reelected in 1991.

Positive Impact

As chief, Mankiller worked hard to find jobs, improve health care, and better the lives of the 95,000-member Cherokee Nation of Oklahoma. She established a community-owned corporation that operates factories, a motel, gift shops, a ranch, a lumber company, and several other businesses. The corporation's income helps pay for health care, job training, a Head Start preschool program, and a high school. In 1994, Wilma Mankiller announced that she would not seek reelection at the end of her term. She cited a passage from the Bible—"To every thing there is a season." Then she added, "My season here is coming to an end."

Mankiller has received many honors, including *Ms.* magazine's Woman of the Year. Recently, she wrote a book about her life, which she titled *Mankiller: A Chief and Her People*. The book contains much Cherokee history, because, Mankiller says, it is such an important part of her life. She strongly encourages young Native Americans to stay in touch with their past.

Oprah Winfrey

This popular talk show host has built a broadcasting empire and gives generously of her fortune to others.

In 1988, Oprah Winfrey and her producers took their cameras to Southwestern High School in Baltimore to explore the topic of school violence.

Early Stages

Oprah Winfrey was born in 1954 in the small Mississippi town of Kosciusko. Her parents, Vernita Lee and Vernon Winfrey, were not married and later separated. When Lee went to Milwaukee to find work, she left Oprah with Grandmother Winfrey. Mrs. Winfrey was a religious woman who taught Oprah the Bible and took her to church. Even after Oprah moved to Milwaukee to be with her mother, her life continued to center on the church.

Troubled Times As a child, Oprah was an avid reader and a good student. She was often asked to recite poetry at church functions. But she was also a rebellious child. Unable to cope with Oprah's misbehavior, Lee sent Oprah to live with Vernon Winfrey in Nashville. Oprah moved back and forth between her parents' homes until, at age 14, she remained with her father. The strict household of Vernon Winfrey imposed a sense of order on Oprah's life. He believed strongly in the value of education and encouraged his daughter to set high standards and goals for herself.

In school, Oprah became involved in public speaking and dramatics. By the time she was a high school senior, she knew that she wanted a career in the performing arts. Winfrey's first professional break came while she was still in high school—a local radio station hired her to read the news. She continued to work in radio after enrolling at Tennessee State University in Nashville. In her sophomore year, she was hired to be a newscaster at a Nashville television station.

While still attending college, Oprah was earning an annual salary of $15,000. A few months before graduation in 1976, she left school to take a job at a Baltimore television station.

A Star Is Born

Winfrey was too emotionally involved with her stories to be a good news reporter. So the station gave her an interview show, which became extremely popular. In 1984, a Chicago TV station hired her to host a talk program called *A.M. Chicago*. The station wanted a personality to compete with Phil Donahue, the host of a successful, nationally aired talk show produced in Chicago. In just two months, her ratings jumped past his. The success of the show led to several important changes.

- The name of the show was changed to *The Oprah Winfrey Show*.
- It was expanded to an hour.
- It was syndicated (sold to other TV stations across the country).

Oprah Winfrey's gift for drama and her poise in front of TV cameras and a live audience were perfectly suited to the talk show format. She had a knack for encouraging guests to reveal things about themselves. She also readily shared her own personal experiences and feelings. Winfrey soon built a devoted national audience.

Oprah and Harpo Winfrey's success was not limited to the small screen. Even though she had had little acting experience, she won a major supporting role in the 1985 movie *The Color Purple.* The movie was based on an Alice Walker novel that focuses on the hardships and triumphs of African American women raised in the rural South. Winfrey was nominated for an Academy Award for her work in the film. The role and the nomination further boosted her popularity—Oprah quickly became a household name.

After her success in Hollywood, Winfrey decided to form her own production company. In addition to producing her television show, Harpo (Oprah spelled backwards) Productions creates television movies and films with spiritual or social messages. One example is *The Women of Brewster Place,* a story of urban black women. It was the highest rated miniseries of the 1988–1989 television season.

More Talk In her talk show, Winfrey likes to address themes that might be ignored otherwise. Once she taped her show in all-white Forsyth County, Georgia, forcing her audience members to face their negative feelings about African Americans. She has interviewed urban gang members, a woman with 92 personalities, and a great-grandmother who gave her house to a family left homeless by Hurricane Andrew.

Sometimes, Oprah's choice of guests has shown questionable judgment. Some critics have said that Winfrey and her producers pursue the most sensationalist, or shocking, stories as well as the highest ratings.

Life at the Top

Interesting topics and a warm personality have helped make Oprah Winfrey the nation's favorite talk show host. She is also one of the world's highest paid entertainers. Her show is seen by over 17 million people a day in 64 countries. Some 90 million people watched her live interview with singer Michael Jackson. Winfrey does more than 200 shows a year. Some people wait more than a year to get a ticket to a studio taping.

Sharing the Wealth Friends and neighbors talk about how down-to-earth Winfrey is. Unchanged by her success, she herself says, "I still have my feet on the ground. I just have better shoes." Once Winfrey sold a pair of those shoes for $675. She gave the money to a high school, then gave the school an additional $1 million. She spends $50,000 a year to provide a meal a day for the people of Alexandra, South Africa. One year at Easter, she made a surprise visit to a church in a run-down district of Los Angeles. The pastor was so flustered

> "Think like a queen. A queen is not afraid to fail. Failure is another stepping-stone to greatness."
>
> —Spelman College Commencement address, 1993

Winfrey is frequently asked to address women's groups. She advises them to aim high.

that he forgot to take up a collection. Winfrey wrote the church a check for $10,000.

Winfrey often speaks to women and young people about empowerment (the ability to accomplish one's own goals) and personal responsibility. In 1988, she gave the commencement address at Tennessee State University and was awarded an honorary college degree in recognition of her accomplishments. In return, she established a scholarship program for ten students a year. Winfrey chooses the recipients and follows their progress. She also gave $1 million to Morehouse College for scholarships and has given millions to the United Negro College Fund.

Winfrey has received numerous awards, including several Emmy Awards, *Ms.* magazine's Woman of the Year, and the Image Award of the National Association for the Advancement of Colored People. Winfrey has built a broadcasting empire out of hard work and the ability to get in touch with people's feelings. She has used the fruits of that success generously to help others.

In 1991, Oprah Winfrey was awarded an Emmy, one of television's highest awards.

43

Glossary

advocate: One who supports or defends a cause or policy, or who pleads on another person's behalf.

American Indian Rights Movement: Movement begun by Native Americans to call attention to their need for better education, health care, and living conditions, and to make the U.S. government honor past treaties.

amnesty: An official pardon, given by a government or a ruler, for offenses committed against the government.

animal behaviorist: A scientist who studies the ways in which animals act in relation to one another and to their environment.

anti-Semitism: Hostility or discrimination against Jews.

aquatic biology: The study of plants and animals that live and grow in water.

assassinate: To murder by surprise attack, especially a politically prominent person.

aviation: The design, production, and operation of aircraft.

botany: The study of plants.

braille: A system of printing and writing for blind people in which letters are indicated by raised dots.

censor: To examine plays, books, movies, newspapers, and other media for the purpose of removing material that is considered to be politically, morally, or otherwise offensive.

chromosome: One of several threadlike structures found in each cell that enable the cell to reproduce itself. Chromosomes contain thousands of genes, which are responsible for inherited characteristics.

circulation department: The department of a newspaper, magazine, or other publication that is concerned with the number of copies issued and the distribution of copies.

contralto: The lowest female singing voice.

contras: Nicaraguan rebels who fought a civil war against the Sandinista government, with support from the U.S. government.

cultural anthropology: The study of human cultures.

DDT: A powerful pesticide that is used to kill mosquitoes and other insects, and that may accumulate in the environment and cause toxic effects in other animal species. DDT was banned in the United States in 1972.

dissent: A difference in thought or opinion; nonconformity.

editorial department: The department of a newspaper, magazine, or other publication that is in charge of collecting and writing the news and expressing opinions.

embargo: A restriction on commerce; a suspension of trade of a particular commodity, such as oil or grain.

empowerment: The ability to accomplish one's goals.

feminist: One who advocates political, economic, and social equality of the sexes and who speaks on behalf of women's rights and interests.

food chain: The succession of plants and animals in an environment that are connected to each other in such a way that each member feeds on the one below it and is itself eaten by the one above it. An example of a food chain is grain-chickens-humans.

freedom of the press: The right to gather and publish information and opinions free of restrictions or fear of punishment by the government. This applies to both printed and broadcast material, including newspapers, books, television, and radio.

genetics: The study of how offspring inherit characteristics from their parents.

guerrilla: A member of a band of independent soldiers, not a part of the regular army, who commit sabotage and attack the enemy unexpectedly.

hospice: An institution that provides treatment and comfort for those who are dying.

impeach: To bring charges against a public official for misconduct while in office.

junta: A council or group of military officials who govern a country after seizing control of the government.

kibbutz: A communal farm settlement in Israel where each member takes turns doing different jobs.

leprosy: A chronic bacterial disease, characterized by skin lesions, that causes disfigurement and nerve paralysis.

missionary: A person who does religious, educational, or charitable work, usually in a foreign country.

monsoon: The wind system that influences climate, especially in southern Asia and India, producing dry and wet seasons. Summer monsoons are characterized by heavy rains.

mutation: A genetic change that occurs from one generation to the next.

Myanmar: The official name given to Burma by General U Ne Win when he seized power in 1962.

nationalist: A person devoted to the interests and culture of his or her own nation; one who supports national independence.

New Deal: The policies of the administration of President Franklin Roosevelt—including social, economic, and political reforms—that were introduced in the 1930s in an effort to help the United States recover from the Great Depression.

Parkinson's disease: A disease of the nervous system that causes uncontrollable shaking.

Pentagon Papers: Documents from a secret Defense Department study of U.S. military involvement in Vietnam.

pesticide: A chemical compound that kills unwanted insects and weeds.

photojournalism: The telling of stories of individuals or events through photographs.

pogrom: An organized massacre of a minority group, especially Jews.

primates: A classification of mammals that includes monkeys, apes, and humans.

Sandinista: A member of Nicaragua's Sandinista National Liberation Front (FSLN), revolutionary guerrilla fighters who succeeded in overthrowing the Somoza government and forming a military, left-wing government.

sari: The traditional dress of Indian women, consisting of a long, bright cloth wrapped around the body.

Sikh: A follower of Sikhism, a religious sect of northwest India. Sikhism is an offshoot of Hinduism that believes in one God and denies the Indian caste system.

Trail of Tears: The westward route taken by the Cherokee Indians in the 1830s after being forced from their land by the U.S. government; so called because 4,000 of 15,000 people died along the way.

treason: The betrayal of one's country by plotting to overthrow the government or by giving aid to the enemy in time of war.

Watergate: A popular name for a political scandal that began in 1972 and resulted in the resignation of President Richard Nixon. The Watergate building in Washington, D.C., was the site of the Democratic National Committee headquarters. A break-in and electronic bugging during the presidential election campaign of 1972, and a subsequent cover-up, were found to involve several Republican Party officials.

Zionism: The plan or movement aimed at reestablishing a Jewish national homeland in Palestine.

Suggested Readings

Note: An asterisk (*) denotes a Young Adult title.

*Blue, Rose, and Nadem, Corinne J. *Barbara Jordan*. Chelsea House, 1992.

*Buffalo, Audreen. *Meet Oprah Winfrey*. Random House, 1993.

*Butler, Francelia. *Indira Gandhi*. Chelsea House, 1986.

Carson, Rachel. *Silent Spring*. Houghton Mifflin, 1987.

*Clucas, Joan G. *Mother Teresa*. Chelsea House, 1988.

*Daffron, Carolyn. *Margaret Bourke-White*. Chelsea House, 1988.

Felsenthal, Carol. *Power, Privilege, and the Post: The Katharine Graham Story*. Putnam, 1993.

*Freedman, Russell. *Eleanor Roosevelt: A Life of Discovery*. Clarion Books, 1993.

Gibson, William. *Miracle Worker*. Bantam, 1989.

Goodall, Jane. *In the Shadow of Man,* rev. ed. Houghton Mifflin, 1983.

*Green, Rayna. *Women in American Indian Society*. Chelsea House, 1992.

*Hoobler, Dorothy, and Hoobler, Thomas. *Italian Portraits*. Images Across the Ages series. Raintree Steck-Vaughn, 1993.

Jackson, Guida M. *Women Who Ruled*. ABC-CLIO, 1990.

Jacobs, William J. *Eleanor Roosevelt: A Life of Happiness and Tears*. Marshall Cavendish, 1991.

Keller, Helen. *The Story of My Life*. Bantam Books, 1990.

*Lauber, Patricia. *Lost Star: The Story of Amelia Earhart*. Scholastic, 1988.

Mankiller, Wilma, and Wallis, Michael. *Mankiller: A Chief and Her People*. St. Martin's, 1992.

*McAuley, Karen. *Golda Meir*. Chelsea House, 1985.

*Patterson, Charles. *Marian Anderson*. Franklin Watts, 1988.

*Rand, Jacki Thompson. *Wilma Mankiller*. American Indian Stories series. Raintree Steck-Vaughn, 1993.

*Randolph, Blythe. *Amelia Earhart*. Marshall Cavendish, 1991.

Read, Phyllis J., and Witlieb, Bernard L. *The Book of Women's Firsts*. Random House, 1992.

*Saw Myat Yin. *Burma*. Marshall Cavendish, 1990.

*Shapiro, Miles. *Maya Angelou*. Chelsea House, 1994.

*Standing, E. M. *Maria Montessori: Her Life and Work*. NAL/Dutton, 1989.

*Stone, Melissa. *Flying High*. Moments in American History series. Raintree Steck-Vaughn, 1989.

*Veglahn, Nancy. *Women Scientists*. Facts on File, 1992.

*Wadsworth, Ginger. *Rachel Carson: A Voice for the Earth*. Lerner, 1991.

*Wepman, Dennis. *Helen Keller*. Chelsea House, 1987.

*Williams, Brian. *Pioneers of Flight*. Raintree Steck-Vaughn, 1990.

*Ziesk, Edra. *Margaret Mead*. Chelsea House, 1990.

Index